Learn to Play
Bass Guitar

Learn to Play
Bass Guitar

Phil Capone

CHARTWELL
BOOKS, INC.

A QUARTO BOOK

Published in 2009 by
Chartwell Books
A division of Book Sales, Inc.
114 Northfield Avenue
Edison, New Jersey 08837
USA

ISBN10: 0-7858-2480-4
ISBN13: 978-0-7858-2480-0
QUAR.PBG

This book was designed and produced by
Quarto Publishing plc
The Old Brewery
6 Blundell Street
London N7 9BH

Project editor: Chloe Todd Fordham
Art editor: Emma Clayton
Designers: Jon Wainwright and Paul Griffin
Photographer: Martin Norris
Technical experts: Richard Jones
        and Leo Coulter
Picture research: Sarah Bell
        and Gwen Campbell
Design assistant: Saffron Stocker
Proofreader: Helen Atkinson
Indexer: Diana LeCore

Art director: Caroline Guest
Creative director: Moira Clinch
Publisher: Paul Carslake

Manufactured by Modern Age Repro House
Ltd, Hong Kong
Printed by Midas Printing International
Limited, China

10 9 8 7 6 5 4 3 2 1

Contents

* For quick reference to the key terms, symbols, and diagrams used in this book, see the fold-out flap, opposite page 254

Introduction

Learning a musical instrument demands dedication and hard work, but that doesn't mean it can't be fun too—in fact, you'll find it's an extremely rewarding experience. But if you're going to teach yourself, you'll need an engaging, easy-to-understand tutor.

The first thing you'll notice about this book is the practical design: it's small enough to pack into your guitar case, the unique spiral-bound format makes it a joy to use, and a useful fold-out flap (which falls opposite page 254 but can stay open at all times until you become more comfortable with reading music) contains an at-a-glance key to understanding bass guitar basics.

Better still, the teaching content has been carefully structured into 29 essential lessons and each one explores new skills while reinforcing previous techniques. As well as conventional TAB, rhythmic notation is provided to ensure that this crucial element of the music is fully understood. Picking and fingerstyle techniques feature throughout, and ideal hand positions and posture are covered during the early chapters to help you avoid bad habits. What's more, technique priming and theory-building lessons culminate in "workout" chapters that feature a full-length original arrangement. You can listen to this on the accompanying CD which you will find at the back of the book. The CD not only includes a full mix featuring drums, guitar and keyboards (providing a realistic and challenging aid to practice), but also a backing track (minus the bass part) so that you can play along. Listening is just as important as practice and you will find reference to essential listening throughout this book, from genre-based discographies to suggestions for downloads, ensuring a holistic approach to learning.

Following the "Lessons" are two invaluable resources: the "Scale library" and the "Arpeggio library" and, last but not least, an unbiased, extensive "Buyer's Guide" that explains the different types of basses, amps, and accessories available. Heck, there's even a chapter on how to pass your first audition! So what are you waiting for? Grab that bass and let's get started...

How to use this book

Learning to play the bass guitar from scratch can be tough: this book is designed to make the process as easy—and as fun!—as possible.

The main part of this book is devoted to "**The Lessons**" (pages 14–165): a series of instructive, interactive tutorials that will get you thinking and playing like a pro in no time.

These panels offer extra information on musical terminology, advice on how to better your playing technique, and suggestions for great downloads.

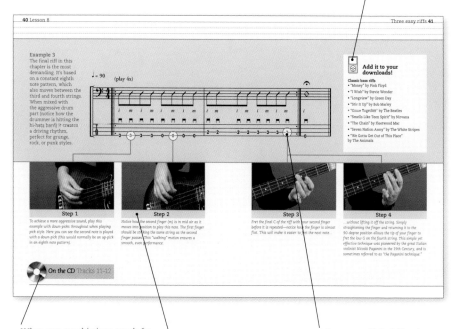

40 Lesson 8

Three easy riffs **41**

Example 3
The final riff in this chapter is the most demanding It's based on a constant eighth note pattern, which also moves between the third and fourth strings. When mixed with the aggressive drum part (notice how the drummer is hitting the hi-hats hard) it creates a driving rhythm, perfect for grunge, rock, or punk styles.

♩ = 90   (play 4x)

Add it to your downloads!

Classic bass riffs
• "Money" by Pink Floyd
• "I Wish" by Stevie Wonder
• "Longview" by Green Day
• "Stir It Up" by Bob Marley
• "Come Together" by The Beatles
• "Smells Like Teen Spirit" by Nirvana
• "The Chain" by Fleetwood Mac
• "Seven Nation Army" by The White Stripes
• "We Gotta Get Out of This Place" by The Animals

Step 1
To achieve a more aggressive sound, play this example with down-picks throughout when playing pick style. Here you can see the second note is played with a down-pick (this would normally be an up-pick in an eighth note pattern)

Step 2
Notice how the second finger (m) is in mid air as it moves into position to play this note. The first finger should be striking the same string as the second finger passes. This "walking" motion ensures a smooth, even performance.

Step 3
Fret the final C of the riff with your second finger before it is repeated—notice how the finger is almost flat. This will make it easier to fret the next note .

Step 4
...without lifting it off the string. Simply straightening the finger and returning it to the 90-degree position allows the tip of your finger to fret the low G on the fourth string. This simple yet effective technique was pioneered by the great Italian violinist Niccolò Paganini in the 19th Century, and is sometimes referred to as "the Paganini technique."

On the CD Tracks 11–12

When you see this icon, reach for the audio CD at the back of the book, scroll to the relevant track numbers, and play along! Where two track numbers are given: the first indicates the full-mix (this is how the example should sound when played correctly); the second is the backing track only.

Step-by-step photographs illustrate the right-hand and left-hand techniques and fingering detail.

All steps are linked directly to the TAB, giving you clear photographic reference at regular, specific points in each musical example, making your journey through the lessons as easy and clear as possible.

The "**Scale library**" (pages 166–215) and "**Arpeggio library**" (pages 216–233) are essential learning for all aspiring bass players.

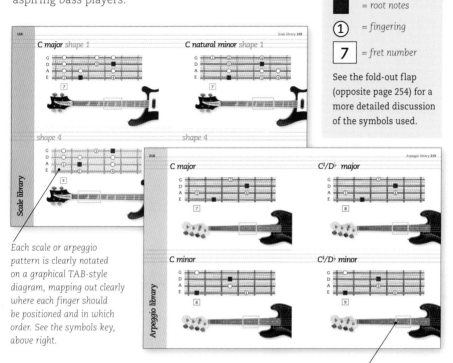

Each scale or arpeggio pattern is clearly notated on a graphical TAB-style diagram, mapping out clearly where each finger should be positioned and in which order. See the symbols key, above right.

Symbol key

■ = root notes

① = fingering

7 = fret number

See the fold-out flap (opposite page 254) for a more detailed discussion of the symbols used.

This handy fretboard locator clearly defines the region of the neck that you should play on.

Notes on the scale library

• To keep things simple, only the two most important shapes out of a possible five in the "CAGED" system (see Glossary on page 250) are given for each scale: shape 1 and 4 (based on open E and A guitar chords respectively).

• Scale fingerings are kept to a minimum to keep the diagram as clear as possible.

• You should play scales strictly "in position"—you will notice (in the shape-1 C major scale on page 168, for example) that fingerings are only annotated as they occur and not repeated. Additional fingerings (as in shape 1 of the C minor scale on page 170) indicate an "out of position" shift part-way through the scale.

⤷ **See also:**
The fold-out flap, which falls opposite page 254

The fingerboard

Finding notes on the fingerboard is not easy;
even some accomplished players who have learnt
"by ear" encounter difficulties. However, there's
really no excuse for vagueness. Other musicians
get frustrated easily if you can't find the root
notes of a chord sequence, and as for transposing
scales, arpeggios, and riffs—forget it! Spend
some time learning the fretboard notes carefully.

The fretboard

*This easy-to-use diagram will help you to understand
how the fretboard works. Begin by memorizing the
notes that fall on the fretboard markers (i.e. third,
fifth, seventh, and ninth frets) and remember that
the entire fingerboard repeats an octave higher from
the twelfth fret.*

Fretboard markers

*The spots that fall on the third, fifth,
seventh, and ninth frets are called
fretboard markers and will help you
find the note you want quickly.*

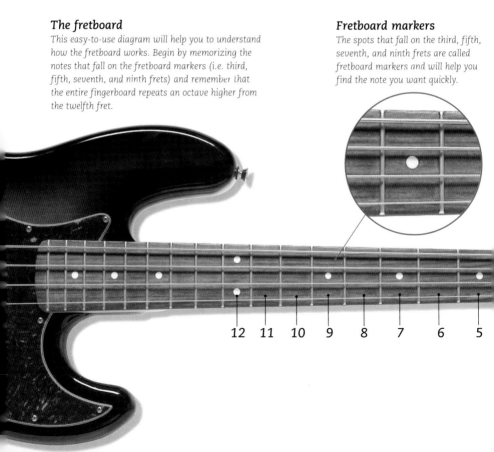

12   11   10   9   8   7   6   5

Fret 1
4 = F
3 = A#/B♭
2 = D#/E♭
1 = G#/A♭

Fret 4
4 = G#/A♭
3 = C#/D♭
2 = F#/G♭
1 = B

Fret 7
4 = B
3 = E
2 = A
1 = D

Fret 10
4 = D
3 = G
2 = C
1 = F

Fret 2
4 = F#/G♭
3 = B
2 = E
1 = A

Fret 5
4 = A
3 = D
2 = G
1 = C

Fret 8
4 = C
3 = F
2 = A#/B♭
1 = D#/E♭

Fret 11
4 = D#/E♭
3 = G#/A♭
2 = C#/D♭
1 = F#/G♭

Fret 3
4 = G
3 = C
2 = F
1 = A#/B♭

Fret 6
4 = A#/B♭
3 = D#/E♭
2 = G#/A♭
1 = C#/D♭

Fret 9
4 = C#/D♭
3 = F#/G♭
2 = B
1 = E

Fret 12
4 = E
3 = A
2 = D
1 = G

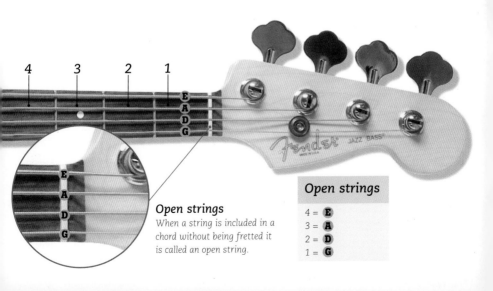

Open strings
When a string is included in a
chord without being fretted it
is called an open string.

Open strings
4 = **E**
3 = **A**
2 = **D**
1 = **G**

Notes for left-handed players

The aspiring left-handed bassist has a dilemma to face: is it best to buy a left-handed instrument, or simply to play right-handed and enjoy the wider choice (and often lower prices) of instruments available to "righties?"

Left vs right

On a conventional bass guitar, the fretting hand is the right hand. This can prove problematic for left-handed players. Some "lefties" will simply opt to play a right-handed guitar. After all, there is no such thing as a left-handed piano. Try a few left-handed and right-handed guitars in a music store before you make your decision. Don't worry if you can't play anything; just sit down with the instrument and pick a couple of open strings. If a left-handed instrument feels more natural to hold, then go with your gut feeling. There are plenty of famous left-handed bassists (Sir Paul McCartney for starters) so you won't be alone if you choose a left-handed model. These are available across all the major manufacturers' ranges.

Adapting a right-handed bass

The alternative is to buy a right-handed bass, flip it upside down, and restring it, but this can cause intonation and tuning problems and you may find it awkward to play when sitting. Furthermore, the cutaway of an electric guitar will be on the wrong side of the neck, making access to high notes difficult. In the long run, it's less hassle to buy a left-handed guitar: all of the key components (the bridge, nut, body, and neck) are reversed to ensure the instrument is comfortable to play and easy to tune. But there are no hard and fast rules. Some players learn to play a right-handed guitar turned upside down without re-stringing! With the high G-string closest to you, everything is, in effect, back to front!

Using this book

As far as reading music goes, the pitches on the stave or TAB don't relate to the guitar visually, so this should present no real problems. Scale and arpeggio diagrams are a little trickier since you will have to reverse the shape or pattern. Don't worry "lefties:" this is not as complicated as it sounds and, with a little practice, you will soon be able to decipher these diagrams with no real difficulty.

The Lessons

From picking up your very first bass guitar to understanding TAB and creating basic bass lines, these 29 easy-to-follow lessons are packed full of essential info, useful tips, and clear step-by-step photography that will have you funking and grooving in no time. Use the audio CD at the back of the book to perfect your intonation and rhythm, or take a brief break from the theory by turning to one of the five "workouts." These interludes fall at random throughout the chapter, and explore in more detail a particular musical genre, such as punk, rock, country, funk, and reggae.

How to hold your bass

There are two ways to hold the bass guitar: standing using a strap, and sitting, with the bass resting on your knee. Most players stand when they're performing at a gig or at a band rehearsal, but for practice sessions at home (or in that mid-tour hotel room), most bassists will prefer to sit.

Standing position

There's no denying it: a low-slung bass looks cool. However, if it hangs too low, you'll find it incredibly difficult to play with any degree of accuracy, and you may even suffer muscular problems as a result of incorrect posture.

At the other extreme were the 1980s slap-bass virtuosos who insisted on wearing their bass so high it could have passed as a neck brace (check out YouTube for the culprits)! So although trends and fashions may dictate a particular height, as with most things, compromise is best.

For ideal posture, position your bass at a slight angle so that the strings cross your body just above belt height, as shown here by Bill Wyman from The Rolling Stones.

Sitting position

This is the most important posture to get right; if you get hooked on bass-playing big-time you could soon find yourself practicing for several hours a day. It's during practice that musicians tend to use the most demanding techniques and repetitive patterns (such as scales and arpeggios), so it's important to get your posture right from the get-go in order to avoid any nasty repetitive strain injuries.

The bass guitar is a heavy and unwieldly beast so you may choose to use a strap when sitting, which can improve your playing position and will take the weight off your leg. Resting the bass on your leg alone is likely to restrict blood flow and lead to "pins and needles," so investing in a good strap may prevent an embarrassing episode with your tour manager: just imagine if he spotted you hobbling around on one leg! Not cool!

Top tip

Spending time on your posture is time well spent. An awkward playing position makes learning hard work and will restrict your rate of progress.

Here Jack Bruce from Cream demonstrates how you can still sit and play while using a strap. The bass is a rare 6-string Fender VI.

Listen up!

Adjusting the strap

Whether you're standing or sitting, it's important to get the length of your strap right. This is much easier to adjust when you're sitting, as you'll have both hands free. If you find you need the strap to be a bit shorter when sitting, mark the strap with a waterproof marker pen at the best sitting and standing lengths.

Getting in tune

For experienced players, the routine of tuning will feel like second nature; for the beginner, however, it can be a confusing and frustrating process. This lesson will show you how to keep your bass in tune with the minimum amount of hassle.

Relative tuning

"I don't understand, it was in tune when I bought it!" This old joke is often wheeled out during rehearsals to excuse an instrument that's slipped horribly out of tune. Relative tuning is one way to ensure that you'll never need to recycle that well-worn phrase.

The process is used to check that all the strings are in tune with each other—useful if you don't have access to a tuner. Use the TAB to your right to check the pitch of each string individually. Sound the notes simultaneously; when the pitches are close you will hear a beating or pulsating effect caused by the difference in pitch. As the pitches get closer, the beating will slow and then disappear altogether when the strings are in tune.

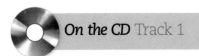

On the CD Track 1

Listen up!

Concert pitch
Concert pitch is a globally recognized system of tuning where the A above middle C (A4) = 440Hz. Science apart, this enables musicians from anywhere in the world to get together and jam without arguing.

1)A

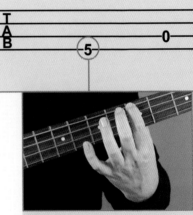

Step 1

Play the first note on the fourth string (the string closest to you) and allow it to ring while you play the second note on the open third (A) string. Your aim is to adjust the tuning of the third string until both notes sound identical, as described on page 21.

▶▶ **See also:** Reading TAB on page 26

Top tip

When you're plugged into an electronic tuner, make sure your volume is fully turned up. If not, you'll get a weak, inaccurate signal that the tuner won't recognize.

2)D   3)G

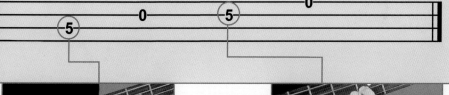

Step 2

Repeat step 1, only this time start on the third string and adjust the tuning of the second (D) string. Don't forget, this step won't work unless the previous step has been carried out correctly! It is worth checking again that the two notes in step 1 sound identical.

Step 3

Repeat step 2, playing the fifth-fret note on the second string and adjusting the tuning of the first (G) string. Don't forget, this step won't work unless the previous two steps have been carried out correctly! Again, you should quickly repeat the previous steps to make sure.

Continued over the page >>>

A note on over-tuning

Don't rely on relative tuning exclusively. Bass guitars have a metal truss rod embedded in their necks (some, like Rickenbackers, have two) to counteract the pressure exerted by the strings. Permanently tuning all the strings sharp or flat to concert pitch will apply too little or too much pressure to the neck, which, over time, can cause it to warp, resulting in permanent damage.

Using a tuner

Electronic tuners are now widely available, very accurate, and relatively cheap. In fact there's really no argument for not buying one. It will help you to keep your instrument in tune and sounding its best. Don't think of an electronic tuner as some kind of cop-out either: all the pros use them; they're extremely efficient; and they allow accurate tuning in noisy environments such as rehearsal rooms and gig venues.

Modern tuners are generally automatic, which means they recognize which string you're playing, so you don't have to fiddle around with any switches. The tuner will indicate with an LED arrow and/or dial reading how sharp or flat the string is, so all you have to do is to make the appropriate adjustments.

There are also many online guitar tuners available (just type "guitar tuner" into Google); some operate

Turn the machine heads clockwise to flatten the note, and counter-clockwise to sharpen the note.

The nut holds the strings in place at the end of the neck. When buying your bass, look for a smooth, cleanly cut nut.

within your browser, others involve downloading software. These virtual tuners work in exactly the same way as the real thing and most are free. The downsides are: portability (even a laptop won't fit in your gig bag); you'll have to boot up your computer each time you want to tune; and you'll need a good quality soundcard installed, which will cost far more than a regular tuner.

⏩ **See also:** Guitar tuners on page 246

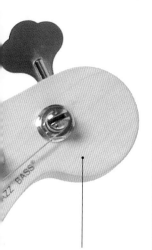

The headstock or peghead holds the bass guitar's strings. They can be straight or angled, depending on the preferred style of the manufacturer and the journey of the strings after they pass the nut.

Making adjustments

Whichever method you use to identify an out of tune string, your next problem is how to get it back in tune. The bass guitar's tuners (called machine heads) are located on the headstock, either as four along the top, or two on each side. Depending on which model you have, identify which machine head belongs to the string you want to adjust (this will soon become second nature) and turn it anti-clockwise to sharpen the pitch or clockwise to flatten it. Always play the note as you're tuning to verify that you're turning the tuner the right way. Usually a fraction of a turn is enough, so don't spin it like a tap!

Step 1

Turn the fourth string's machine head anti-clockwise to sharpen (raise) the pitch. Remember: a fraction of a turn is usually all that is necessary.

Step 2

Turn the first string's machine head clockwise to flatten (lower) the pitch. When the machine heads are on opposing sides, the tuner is upside down so it may seem like you're turning it anti-clockwise.

The right-hand position

The strings are played using either a pick (plectrum) or fingers. Generally speaking, the pick technique creates a brighter sound with more attack; picking the strings with the fingers creates a warmer, more organic sound and is the preferred technique of many players. Both have their merits, and we'll be exploring these options in more detail in Lesson 7 (page 32).

The pick technique

The first thing to get yourself is a nice thick pick—it's no good trying to play with one of those flimsy bits of plastic that guitarists use! The key to successful picking is to hold the pick firmly enough so that you don't drop it, but loose enough to enable it to move quickly across the strings.

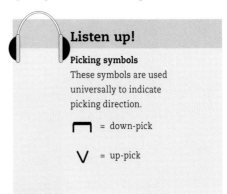

Listen up!

Picking symbols
These symbols are used universally to indicate picking direction.

⊓ = down-pick

V = up-pick

Holding the pick

Hold the pick firmly between your thumb and index finger. Don't allow too much of the pick to protrude from your fingers as this will make it difficult to control as you play.

Positioning the hand

Many bass players "anchor" their hand on the body of the instrument by gently resting on the scratchplate below the strings. This helps to keep your hand in position when playing.

Alternate picking

Here, the pick is poised to play the third string with an up-stroke. A good picking technique demands a mixture of down and up-picks, and this method is known as alternate picking.

▸▸ **See also:** Pick vs fingerstyle on page 32

The finger technique

This technique involves dragging the index (i) or middle (m) finger of your right hand across the string to make it ring. You will achieve greater speed and dexterity by using both fingers.

Listen up!

Finger symbols

Traditional Spanish names are used to name the right-hand fingers—numbers would confuse instructions to the fretting hand.

i (*indice*) = index

m (*medio*) = middle

Picking kings

- John Deacon (Queen)
- Mike Dirnt (Green Day)
- Lemmy (Motorhead)
- Paul McCartney (The Beatles, Wings)
- John Myung (Dream Theatre)
- Krist Novoselic (Nirvana)
- Noel Redding (The Jimi Hendrix Experience)
- Chris Squire (Yes)
- Roger Waters (Pink Floyd)
- Bill Wyman (The Rolling Stones)

Fingerstyle bassists

- Jack Bruce (Cream)
- Cliff Burton (Metallica)
- Geezer Butler (Black Sabbath)
- Sheryl Crow
- Gail Ann Dorsey (David Bowie)
- Flea (Red Hot Chili Peppers)
- Pino Palladino (The Who, John Mayer)
- Jaco Pastorius (Weather Report, solo artist)
- John Paul Jones (Led Zeppelin)

Thumb position

Rest your thumb on the top edge of the middle pick-up to anchor your hand in position. It's important to keep your hand as still as possible when playing the strings.

First finger stroke

Avoid slapping the finger on the string or plucking upward as a fingerstyle guitarist would: keep the first joint of your finger straight, brush it across the fourth string, and rest it on the string below.

Second finger stroke

Here, the second finger is poised to play the third string. The first finger remains at rest on the fourth string (notice how the first finger is bending from the second joint only).

The left-hand position

Developing an efficient left-hand technique should be one of your main priorities. Polished performances will only occur when you can play with the maximum economy of movement, and if you're struggling to fret the notes, you won't be able to concentrate on the music.

Putting in the practice

The professionals make it look so easy, but it's not because they have some special gift; they've just spent years honing and perfecting their technique. One thing's for sure, if you don't make a conscious effort to develop a rock-solid left-hand technique from the start, you're likely to join the ranks of guitarists who have had to frustratingly back-track and re-work their skills. Don't be discouraged when your fingers don't always do what you want them to—good technique is only achieved by sustained, regular practice, so be patient!

Finding the right fingers

Keep these three points in mind when working on your left-hand technique, and you won't go wrong.

The thumb

Your thumb should be positioned in the center of the neck—this will provide maximum support for the fingers when you're pressing down on those strings. Be sure to keep your palm off the neck too!

▶▶ **See also:** The right-hand position on page 22

Top tip

Always try to keep your left-hand thumb pointing upwards on the back of the neck and your fingers hovering over the strings.

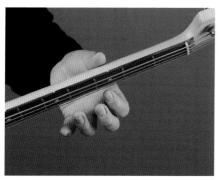

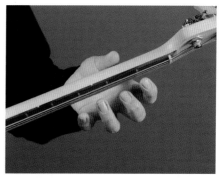

The fingertips

The tip of your finger should approach the fretboard directly from above and ideally at a 90-degree angle (to avoid damping adjacent strings). It's important to place your finger close to the fret to avoid weak, "buzzy-sounding" notes.

The fingers

Aim to keep your fingers hovering above the strings when they're not fretting. This cuts down the movement required and means you will be able to fret notes more easily.

Listen up!

Finger symbols

Only the fingers of the left hand are allocated numbers, since the thumb is not used:

1 = first (index) finger

2 = second (middle) finger

3 = third (ring) finger

4 = fourth (pinky) finger

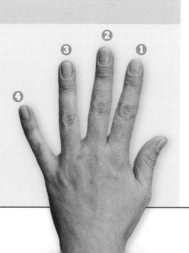

Reading TAB

TAB is short for tablature, a simplified system of notation that's used for bass and guitar. It dates back to the Renaissance (1400–1600) when it was used to notate lute music and today it's used in music magazines, tuition books, and music colleges worldwide. Its format is intuitive and easy to decipher: four lines (called a stave) symbolize the strings of the bass, and the numbers indicate the frets.

Rhythmic notation

TAB, like anything that has been simplified, can have its limitations; the lack of rhythm and fingering indication make it a sketchy guide at best. To remedy this, a conventional stave of music is traditionally added, appearing as an extra stave above the TAB. This is known as rhythmic notation, a system (widely used for guitar and keyboard parts) that uses characters adapted from conventional notation. Since there is no pitch to indicate, the "noteheads" (diamonds or diagonal slashes) always fall on the middle line of the stave. In this book, only rhythmic notation is used to avoid confusion. Once you've got the hang of rhythmic notation, you'll be halfway to getting conventional notation licked.

Example 1
This example TABs two notes on the fourth string (the closest string to you when you're holding the bass). The first note is played open (0 = open string), and the second on the third fret (3 = third fret). Easy!

Example 2
Often bass players are required to play two notes together, known as a double stop. Double stops are written as "stacked" numbers on the TAB. Here, the open first string and open second string are played together.

Example 3
This example of rhythmic notation illustrates the different types of notes that you will encounter throughout this book. Rhythmic notation describes the rhythm without the pitch information.

Example 4
Music is not just about making noise; silence is important too! This example illustrates the equivalent rest symbols for the notes in Example 3. The symbols are identical in both rhythmic and conventional notation.

Top tip

Rhythm is 50% of music. You can have music without pitch, but not without rhythm. Take time to clap through the rhythm first—that's 50% of the job done!

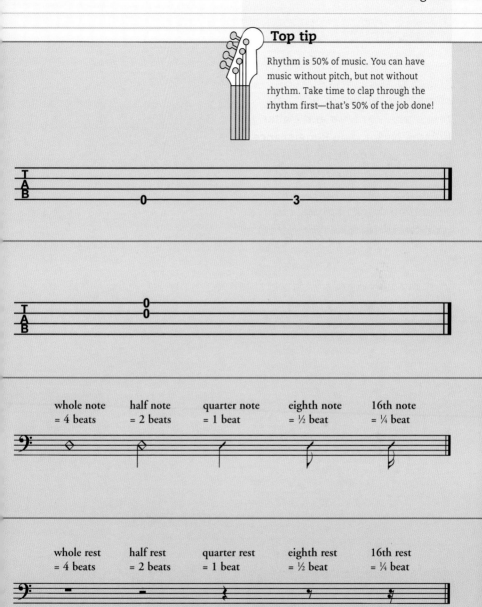

whole note	half note	quarter note	eighth note	16th note
= 4 beats	= 2 beats	= 1 beat	= ½ beat	= ¼ beat

whole rest	half rest	quarter rest	eighth rest	16th rest
= 4 beats	= 2 beats	= 1 beat	= ½ beat	= ¼ beat

Locking with the drums

The bass guitarist is a team player, joining forces with the drummer to provide a solid foundation for the rest of the band to build on. It goes without saying that you'll need to start listening to what drummers do, and in particular to which beats they play their kick drum on. Listen out for how the bass player interacts with the drums—are they copying the kick pattern, weaving around it, or just sticking to a constant pulse?

Keeping time

It's essential to develop a strong sense of time. This doesn't just mean the ability to play rhythms accurately; you must learn to maintain a steady tempo that doesn't speed up or slow down. In short, a bass player needs to be rock solid! Playing along with the CD is a great way to start developing this essential skill.

Example 1

In this example, you'll play half notes on beats one and three. Before you pick up your bass, just clap along to the backing track while counting "one, two, three, four" to make sure you play on the correct beats. When you're playing the notes, allow them to ring for their full value—there should be no gaps!

Step 1

Pick the notes using down-picks only. Notice that the pick should make contact with the string at 90-degrees. Remember to anchor your fingers on the scratchplate.

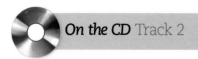

On the CD Track 2

▸▸ **See also:** Three easy riffs on page 36

Top tip

Tapping your foot to a quarter note pulse may feel like rubbing your stomach and patting your head, but it internalizes the pulse, and you will relate to the music in a physical way.

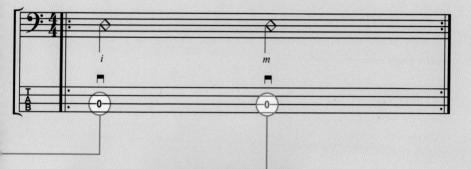

Step 2

Alternate your fingers when you're playing fingerstyle (this is indicated by the "i" and "m" symbols). Here, the open third string is played with the second finger on beat three. Aim to keep your first finger joints straight but not rigid.

Continued over the page >>>

Example 2

Clap this rhythm and it should sound identical to example 1; this is because a clap is a percussive sound—it does not sustain. The example on the CD will reveal a marked difference due to the rests on the second and third beats. The bass notes are damped on these beats, providing space for the drummer's snare, allowing the drums to "breathe."

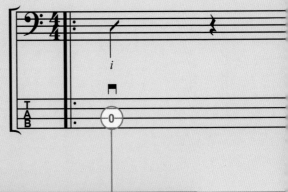

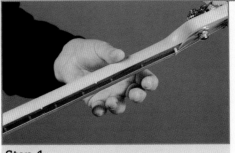

Step 1

Keep your left-hand fingers hovering above the second fret as you play the first note: they need to be in position ready to damp the strings on the second beat.

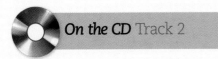

On the CD Track 2

Top tip

It's well worth investing in a metronome. This invaluable tool will ensure you're always practicing to a constant tempo.

Listen up!

Time signatures
You may have noticed a "4/4" at the beginning of the line of rhythmic notation. This is called a time signature and, in this case, it means there are four beats in a bar at the end of which a bar line (a single vertical line) is drawn. The first beat in a bar is called the downbeat; it is the strongest beat in a bar. Think of notes on the downbeat as reassuring milestones on your musical journey—when you arrive at one, give it some extra "oomph!"

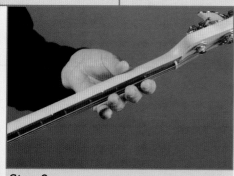

Step 2

Stop the string from ringing by lightly touching it (don't fret it) with your first three fretting-hand fingers. To avoid sounding any notes, the fingers should fall flat across the strings.

Listen up!

Eighth notes
When written individually, eighth notes (or quavers) look just like quarter notes, but with a "tail" at the end of the stem (see page 27). When there are two or more adjacent eighth notes, it is conventional to omit the tail and "beam" the notes together.

Pick vs fingerstyle

In this lesson, you'll learn two short basslines that illustrate the differences between two right-hand techniques: picking and fingerstyle. Generally speaking, the pick is more suited to rock styles (particularly punk and heavy metal) where it facilitates the playing of constant eighth notes with ease. However, many rock and heavy metal players still choose to play with their fingers, so keep an open mind!

Picking the right method

Both examples here incorporate eighth-note rhythms, so make sure you clap through each example first. Listen to the CD (full mix and backing track), but don't expect to be able to play along instantly. Start practicing below the target tempo (see the "Basic tempo markings" table on page 49) and build speed gradually to ensure accuracy and avoid hasty mistakes. When you feel comfortable with the rhythm, begin to alternate fingerstyle and pick technique. Although one may seem more natural to you than the other, persevere with both, at least until you've worked through this book.

Example 1
This is a simple but effective bassline that is centered around a low G on the fourth string. Playing this with the fingers creates a warmer sound than a pick would. Remember that eighth notes last half a beat each, so they normally occur in pairs (or with an eighth rest). To play them accurately you should count "+" between each beat, as illustrated.

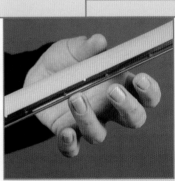

Step 1
Damping a fretted note is quite easy; all you need to do is release the pressure of your fretting hand slightly (without taking it off the string).

On the CD Tracks 3–4

▸▸ **See also:** The right-hand position on page 22

Top tip

Keep tapping your foot when you're counting eighth notes. Your foot should maintain a steady quarter-note pulse. The "+" (offbeat) should then coincide with each up movement of your foot.

Step 2

After plucking the lowest string, each finger should come to rest on the anchored thumb. The photo shows the position of the first (i) finger after playing the first note in the second bar.

Continued over the page >>>

Example 2

This is a constant eighth note pattern, and you will achieve a bright sound with plenty of attack when you play with a pick. Picking helps the bassline to cut through a mix—particularly useful in rock where the guitar is usually distorted. Notice the use of constant alternate picking. You'll need to practice this one slowly before you play along to the CD.

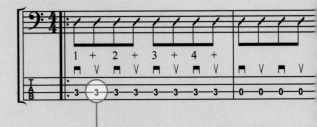

Step 1

The up-picked notes in the first bar should hit the string with the pick at 90-degrees to the string; this will achieve a big, full sound. Keep the sweep of your pick to a minimum and it will be easier to control.

On the CD Tracks 5–6

Listen up!

Metronome markings

In this example, you'll notice a quarter note followed by an equals sign and a number. This indicates the tempo in BPM (beats per minute). You can use the BPM as a target for practice. For example: start practicing at a lower value on your metronome, gradually increasing the tempo each day until you reach your goal.

$$\text{♩} = 75$$

Step 2

When you're playing the open string, keep your third finger hovering above the third fret, ready for the next fretted note.

Three easy riffs

Riffs are a prerequisite of blues, essential in rock, deep and low in reggae, and adopted by the horns in jazz. You'll even find riffs in classical music, where they are given a slightly more technical name: the ostinato.

What is a riff?

A riff is essentially a short, catchy phrase, typically 2–4 bars long, that is repeated continually to form an accompaniment in part of the song's structure (the verse, chorus, or solo for example). In blues, the riff is often used for the whole song.

Riffing on the bass

Most people associate riffs with electric guitar: the sole province of the archetypal guitar hero—all hair and low-slung guitar—belting out a powerful riff to a spellbound audience. What they don't realize is that the riff is probably being played in unison by the bass player, whose job is to double-up the riff and "fatten up" the sound while the guitarist steals the show. But those powerful, deep notes that hit you in the chest at gigs are quite capable of sustaining a riff without the guitarist's help. Turn to page 41 for some examples of killer bass riffs.

On the CD Tracks 7–8

Example 1

This is a funky, pop-style bass riff played entirely on the fourth string. The only difference in the second bar is that the last two notes (G and A) are doubled and played as pairs of eighth notes—an example of how a little rhythmic variation can transform a simple musical idea into a two-bar riff.

Step 1
Keep your first and third fingers hovering above the frets in third position throughout (your first finger above the third fret and your third above the fifth). This way you can play the entire riff without changing your left-hand position.

▶▶ **See also:** Creating walking bass lines on page 126

Top tip

The instruction "play 4x" indicates
that you play the first two bars in each
example four times. So each example is
actually 13 bars long, giving you plenty
of time to get into the groove!

(play 4x)

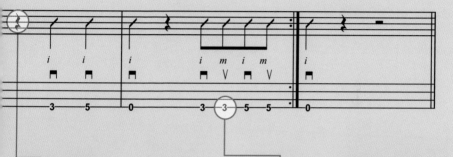

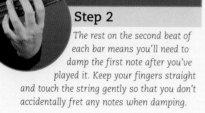

Step 2

*The rest on the second beat of
each bar means you'll need to
damp the first note after you've
played it. Keep your fingers straight
and touch the string gently so that you don't
accidentally fret any notes when damping.*

Step 3

*Alternate right-hand fingers
are only used in the second bar.
Notice the second (m) finger,
poised to strike the second G (third
fret) on the third beat, and how the first
finger is at rest on the thumb after playing
the previous note.*

Continued over the page >>>

Example 2

This is a classic rock-style riff with a 16ths hi-hat groove. Notice how the drum part has no snare; there's just a kick drum on the first and third beats of each bar. The bass adds a quarter note pulse to the drummer's busy hi-hat pattern, creating a driving groove with plenty of space. This would work well in a verse or at the start of a guitar solo.

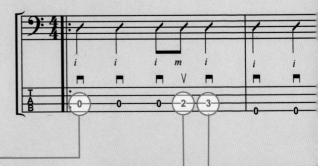

Step 1

Because the lowest note is on the second fret, this riff can be played in second position (i.e. with the first finger above the second fret). As in the previous example, keep the fingers hovering close to the frets while playing the open strings.

Step 2

Here, the second finger frets the final C in the first bar; notice how the first finger is still pressing down on the second fret. Don't waste time lifting your finger off the string if the next note is above it on the same string.

On the CD Tracks 9–10

Listen up!

Fermata sign
The fermata symbol is placed above a note when it should be allowed to ring beyond its normal value. So, the last note in both examples 1 and 2 should be allowed to ring until the note fades.

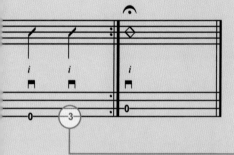

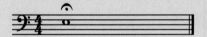

Step 3

Alternate right-hand fingers are only used for the eighth notes in the first bar. Strike your second (m) finger on the second note on the third beat. Keep your first finger at rest on the fourth string after playing the previous note.

Step 4

As you're playing this riff in second position, play all the notes on the third fret with your second finger.

Continued over the page >>>

Example 3

The final riff in this chapter is the most demanding. It's based on a constant eighth-note pattern, which also moves between the third and fourth strings. When mixed with the aggressive drum part (you will notice the drummer is hitting the hi-hats hard on the CD) it creates a driving rhythm perfect for grunge, rock, or punk.

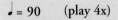

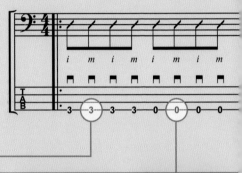

Step 1

To achieve a more aggressive sound, play this example with down-picks throughout when playing pickstyle. Here you can see the second note is played with a down-pick (this would normally be an up-pick in an eighth-note pattern).

Step 2

Notice how the second finger (m) is in mid air as it moves into position to play this note. The first finger should be striking the same string as the second finger passes. This "walking" motion ensures a smooth, even performance.

On the CD Tracks 11–12

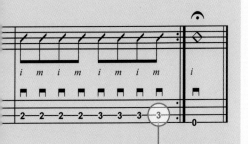

Add it to your downloads!

Classic bass riffs
- "Money" by Pink Floyd
- "I Wish" by Stevie Wonder
- "Longview" by Green Day
- "Stir It Up" by Bob Marley
- "Come Together" by The Beatles
- "Smells Like Teen Spirit" by Nirvana
- "The Chain" by Fleetwood Mac
- "Seven Nation Army" by The White Stripes
- "We Gotta Get Out of This Place" by The Animals

Step 3

Fret the final C of the riff with your second finger before it is repeated—notice how the finger is almost flat. This will make it easier to fret the next note...

Step 4

...without lifting it off the string. Simply straightening the finger and returning it to the 90-degree position allows the tip of your finger to fret the low G on the fourth string. This simple yet effective technique was pioneered by the great Italian violinist Niccolò Paganini in the 19th Century, and is sometimes referred to as "the Paganini technique" (see the glossary on page 250 for more details).

Jumping the strings

Playing on just one or two strings would severely restrict your note choices. In this lesson, you'll be maxing up your technique to incorporate string jumps, which involves skipping over the lower strings to quickly grab a high note in the same position on the neck.

Creating a full sound

If you're playing low G on the fourth string, and you want to incorporate the note an octave higher (that's the same pitch eight notes above), you will have to move a long way to reach it on the same string—all the way up to the fifteenth fret in fact! This can sound cool if you're sliding up to the note for dramatic effect (at the climatic point of a rock tune for example), but it's no good for creating an agile sixteenth-note groove in a funk song. Jumping strings is not exclusive to funk; it's found in just about every genre including rock. For evidence, check out John Paul Jones' nippy octave riffs (played fingerstyle) in the mighty Led Zep's "Immigrant Song."

Example 1

Listen carefully to the backing track to hear how this part locks with the drummer's kick drum. This two-bar pattern adds an octave A note on the fourth beat of the second bar. The "let ring" instruction (see page 45) means that this note should be allowed to ring into the repeat.

Step 1

When playing fingerstyle, play this note with your second finger (m), anchoring your thumb on the pick-up.

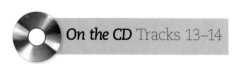

On the CD Tracks 13–14

Top tip

Practice this without the backing track first. Don't worry if it takes a few days or even a week to get the part up to tempo. It's better to play slowly and accurately than to rush and play the wrong notes.

(play 4x)

let ring

Step 2

When playing with a pick, play this note with an up-pick.

Step 3

Fret the octave A with your first finger. Keep it pressed down as long as possible to allow the note to ring into the repeat.

Continued over the page >>>

Example 2

This is a more complex version of the previous example; it's the same drum groove but the bass riff includes higher notes. As in the previous example, these notes should be allowed to "let ring" by keeping the fingers pressed down for as long as possible.

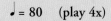

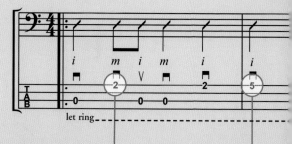

Step 1

Once your first finger has played the low A, skip your second finger (m) across the second string in preparation for the octave on the second beat.

Step 2

If you're using a pick, play the octave jump on the second beat with alternate picking.

Step 3

Fret the high C on the first string with your third finger. This should remain pressed down until you replay the note after the following low A.

On the CD Tracks 15–16

Listen up!

"Let ring"

This instruction usually appears below the stave (or TAB). It indicates that the notes should be allowed to ring into each other and should not be damped. It's important to keep your fingers pressed down for fretted notes for as long as possible.

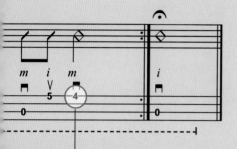

let ring - ⌐

Step 4

By moving your hand slightly you can also fret the high B note with the third finger. This leaves your first finger free for the following high A when repeating.

Listen up!

Dotted notes

A dot placed after any note or rest increases its value by half. The dotted quarter notes below last for one and a half beats. Dotted quarter notes are almost always preceded or followed by an eighth note, as shown here.

Continued over the page >>>

Example 3

The low note was always an open string in the previous examples. Here, the string jump is based on fretted notes, which creates a different sound. Because both notes are fretted, it's much easier to prevent them from ringing together, which is ideal for creating funkier grooves. Both hands are equally busy, so start well below the target tempo.

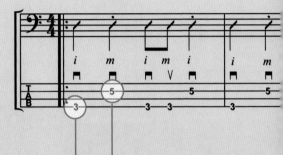

♩ = 80   (play 4x)

Step 1

While fretting the low G with your first finger, your third finger should already be hovering above the fifth fret ready to play the octave. It is perfectly acceptable to use your pinky (fourth finger) if you find this is too much of a stretch.

Step 2

The second note is marked with a staccato dot (see above right) and should be played short. To damp it, release the pressure of your fretting finger slightly (without lifting it off the string). The damping should occur as soon as you've played the string.

On the CD Tracks 17–18

Listen up!

Staccato notes

When a note should be played short (i.e. staccato), a dot is placed above the notehead. Open strings will need to be damped with the left-hand fingers; fretted notes should be cut short by releasing fretting hand pressure.

normal notes - - - - - - staccato - - - - - - - - -

Step 3

Move your first finger down the string while playing the open E. This will ensure the finger is in position for the low F on the first fret and avoid any unmusical "gaps" in your performance.

Step 4

As soon as you've played the low F, release the pressure of the finger (don't take it off the string completely) and slide it back up to the third fret ready for the next note. The slide should be silent: trace the string with your finger like a guide rail.

Playing the offbeats

Offbeats are the notes that fall in the gaps: the "+" parts of each beat when you're counting "1 + 2 + 3 + 4 +" or, to think of it another way, where your foot is in the air if you're tapping along to the groove. The process of emphasizing these so-called "weak" beats has its own musical term: syncopation. Syncopation is a double-edged sword; it makes music more exciting for the listener (or dancer), but harder for the musician to play.

Why play offbeats?

"Okay, so I've already played notes that fall on a '+' in the previous chapter, so what?" This may be true, but they weren't preceded by rests or tied notes, and that's a different kettle of fish altogether! By obscuring the downbeat, the offbeat is accented and a groove is created. If every note fell on the beat, music would be very boring! So it's every budding musician's duty to develop a strong grasp of offbeats—and that includes you, bass players!

Example 1
Practiced daily, this useful warm-up exercise will help you to build a solid understanding of onbeats and offbeats. Start with your metronome set to 60 bpm and don't increase the tempo until you can clap through comfortably, counting the beats as indicated. When you repeat, remember that the last offbeat note will be very close to the quarter note that follows.

Top tip

An old adage goes: "if you can't clap it, you can't play it." How can you expect to master a tricky rhythm if you're worrying about which fingers to use? Play the above example with open strings first.

▸▸ **See also:** Locking with the drums on page 28

Top tip

The ability to play offbeats as confidently as onbeats will take time, so don't get frustrated. Remember that music is hard and it takes constant practice to master new concepts, so be patient.

1   +   2   +   3   +   4   +   1   +   2   +   3   +   4   +

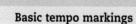

Listen up!

Basic tempo markings

Musical Term	Definition	Metronome Marking
Larghissimo; adagissimo; lentissimo	Extremely slow	40
Largo; adagio; lento	Very slow	40
Larghetto; adagietto	Fairly slow	40
Andante; andantino	Moderately slow	60
Moderato	Moderately	60
Allegretto	Fairly fast	60
Allegro	Fast, quick	120
Vivace; vivo; presto	Quite fast	120
Allegrissimo; vivacissimo; prestissimo	Very fast	208

Continued over the page >>>

Example 2

This may look like a simple bassline, but looks can be deceptive! After the first note, the next time you'll play on the beat will be the third beat of the second bar. Clap this through carefully, making sure you count and tap your foot as you clap. As with most heavily syncopated grooves, the drummer's kick drum fattens the bassline by accenting the same offbeats.

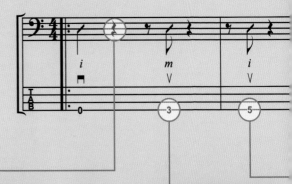

Step 1

Don't forget: a rest means silence, so damp those strings! Gently touch the strings on the second beat to damp the fourth string.

Step 2

When playing with a pick, you should play this note (low G) with an up-pick since it falls on the offbeat. Don't forget: it's important to keep your picking hand anchored by gently resting the fingers on the scratchplate, as shown.

On the CD Tracks 19–20

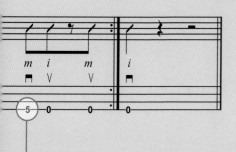

Listen up!

Fingertip tip
Always position your fingertips close to the fret. For example, if you are playing a G (third fret) on the fourth string, place your fingertip in between the second and third frets and as close to the third fret as possible. This technique will make it easier to hold down the note and achieve a clearer sound.

Step 3

Keep your fretting hand in third position throughout.

Step 4

When you're playing fingerstyle, play this note with your second finger (m).

Continued over the page >>>

Example 3

This one is a little tricky, so practice it well below the target tempo at first. Because all of the notes are off the beat it's very easy to lose your place, so count carefully, clapping along with the CD. Once you can play it with the backing track, see if you can just "feel it" without having to count.

Step 1

This example should be played in second position. Fret this note (C) with your second finger, keeping the note short by releasing the finger (without taking it off the string) as soon as you've played it.

Step 2

To emphasize the offbeats it's sometimes a good idea to use down-picks where you would normally pick up.

On the CD Tracks 21–22

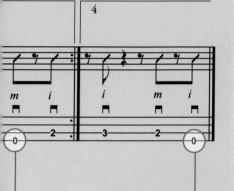

Listen up!

First and second time endings

First and second time endings are very common. On the first play-through, play the "first time" bar as it's called. After the repeat, skip this bar and jump straight to the "second time" ending. In example 3, play the "first time" bar three times (1,2,3), taking the "second time" ending the fourth time through (4).

Step 3

As there is little audible difference between your first or second finger when playing fingerstyle, use strict alternate fingering to keep the performance slick and smooth.

Step 4

Keep the final open E note short by damping it with the left-hand fingers as shown. On the backing track this note is emphasized with a "choked" cymbal hit.

11 Rock workout

The term "rock" is used to describe a wide range of styles, from the detuned power chords of thrash metal, to the gentle harmonies of soft rock. In fact, rock has spawned more sub-genres than any other form of music.

The popularity of rock music has been in decline since the beginning of the decade, partly due to the fact that the newest sub-genres are less mainstream, and partly due to the rise in popularity of hip-hop and R&B. Many new bands fall generally into the "revival" movements, borrowing their styles from the original 1960s and 1970s pioneers. So it's no wonder that the appetite for "classic rock" remains whet, with albums from the music's heyday still selling worldwide and many of the artists (some of whom are still with us) continuing to produce new music and performing worldwide—The Rolling Stones and The Who being two notable examples.

The familiar riffs of conventional rock have influenced various contemporary musicians, like James Hetfield, the lead singer of Metallica.

▶▶ **See also:** Funk workout on page 144

Add it to your downloads!

The role of the bass in rock

Rock is a guitar-dominated music usually played by a group of four musicians (typically: guitar, bass guitar, drums, and vocals), although a band of five is equally common (just add a second guitarist or keyboard player). The bass player's job is the same in every sub-genre of rock: to outline the chord sequence of the song, simultaneously locking with the drummer to create a powerful, driving groove.

Guitar solos feature prominently in rock, but they rarely extend to include the bass player, except in progressive rock styles. Basslines are usually simplistic; they either double the guitar riff or simply pump out the lowest notes of the guitar chords. This doesn't mean that playing the bass guitar in a rock band isn't going to be fun—it's probably the most exciting thing you can do with your clothes on!

The Jimi Hendrix Experience
Axis: Bold As Love
This seminal album was the band's second release and showcases some superb bass-playing by the late Noel Redding.

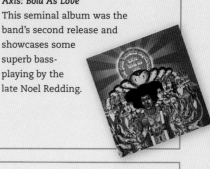

Cream
Disraeli Gears
Cream's second album captures the world's first supergroup at the top of their game. It features powerful bass riffs, wild drum grooves, and soaring guitar solos.

Led Zeppelin
Zeppelin II
Led Zep's follow-up to their hugely successful debut includes the classic "Whole Lotta Love," plus John Paul Jones' stunning bass solo in "The Lemon Song."

Continued over the page >>>

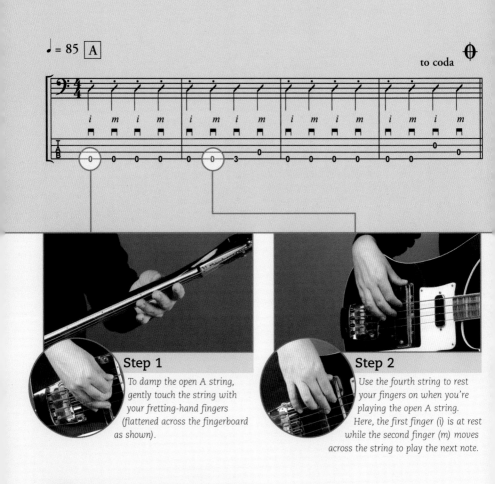

♩ = 85 **A**

to coda

i   m   i   m | *i   m   i   m* | *i   m   i   m* | *i   m   i   m*

Step 1

To damp the open A string, gently touch the string with your fretting-hand fingers (flattened across the fingerboard as shown).

Step 2

Use the fourth string to rest your fingers on when you're playing the open A string. Here, the first finger (i) is at rest while the second finger (m) moves across the string to play the next note.

On the CD Tracks 23–24

Listen up!

The rock bass

The most popular bass guitar in rock music is unquestionably the Fender Precision Bass. Since its introduction in 1951, this instrument has appeared on more famous recordings and performances than any other. Notable runners-up include the Rickenbacker 4001 and the Gibson EB-3.

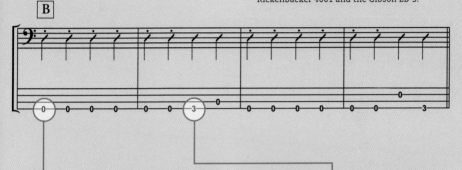

Step 3

For pickstyle, play all the notes in the "A" and "B" sections with down-picks.

Step 4

Fret the low G (third fret note) on the fourth string with the third finger. Make sure you lift the finger off the fretboard before playing the following open third string.

Continued over the page >>>

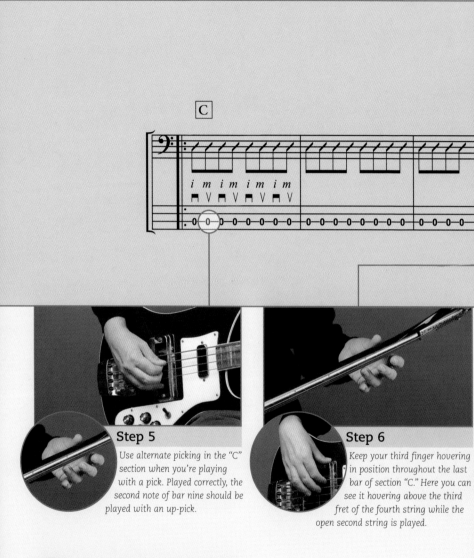

Step 5

Use alternate picking in the "C" section when you're playing with a pick. Played correctly, the second note of bar nine should be played with an up-pick.

Step 6

Keep your third finger hovering in position throughout the last bar of section "C." Here you can see it hovering above the third fret of the fourth string while the open second string is played.

On the CD Tracks 23–24

D.C. al coda

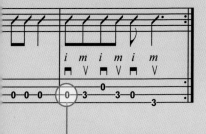

Listen up!

Rehearsal letters

The letters in boxes at the beginning of each new section are called rehearsal letters. They are added to make (yes you've guessed it!) rehearsing easier. You'll find that they also simplify the learning process—you could sum up this arrangement as being:

$$A + B + C + A$$

D.C. al coda

D.C. means Da Capo: an instruction to return to the beginning of the music. It is often followed by "al Coda:" an instruction to jump to the coda (ending) when you see the coda symbol (see below). The coda symbol is always placed at the end of the last bar and at the start of the ending bar(s). So here you would play the first two bars, repeat the first, then jump to the end.

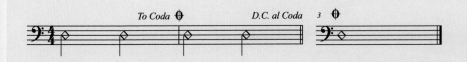

The major scale explained

The major scale is the most important scale in Western music. Master this and in time you will understand how melodies, chords, and arpeggios are constructed.

The role of the bass
"But I'm a bass player, why do I need to learn about chords and arpeggios?" Chords are seldom played on the bass, but it's your job to provide an effective harmonic outline of a given chord sequence. Knowing which notes make up a chord gives you a choice of notes to play in your chosen bassline.

Listen up!

Major scale construction
The interval formula for the major scale produces a specific pattern of whole steps and half steps. Notice how the half steps fall between the third and fourth steps and the seventh and octave—this gives the major scale its distinctive "major" sound.

W = whole step (2 frets or *tone*)

H = half step (1 fret or *semitone*)

1 – 2 – 3 – 4 – 5 – 6 – 7 – Oct

W W H W W W H

Example 1
This one-octave moveable shape involves playing all the fifth fret notes with your fourth finger. You may find it awkward using your pinky, so practice regularly. No rhythm is indicated, so play all the notes evenly at first, and then practice with a metronome. Think of the notes as quarter notes at 60 bpm.

Step 1
Start the scale with your second finger playing the low G on the fourth string. Try to keep your remaining fingers spread out as shown, hovering above the note that they will be required to play.

▶▶**See also:** The natural minor scale on page 92

Top tip

The scales have been tabbed ascending only but you should practice them ascending and descending without repeating the top note. Use the same fretting-hand fingering.

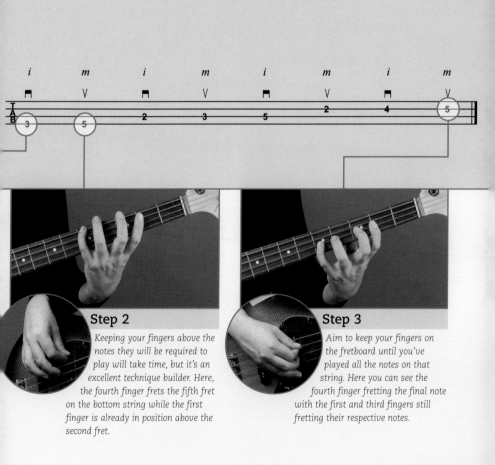

Step 2

Keeping your fingers above the notes they will be required to play will take time, but it's an excellent technique builder. Here, the fourth finger frets the fifth fret on the bottom string while the first finger is already in position above the second fret.

Step 3

Aim to keep your fingers on the fretboard until you've played all the notes on that string. Here you can see the fourth finger fretting the final note with the first and third fingers still fretting their respective notes.

Continued over the page >>>

Example 2

The full two-octave major scale pattern adds the upper octave to the previous example. This involves playing a succession of notes on the first string, which is executed by shifting swiftly up the neck using only your first and third fingers (see steps 3 and 4 below). Being able to play notes along one string smoothly and accurately is a very useful technique to develop.

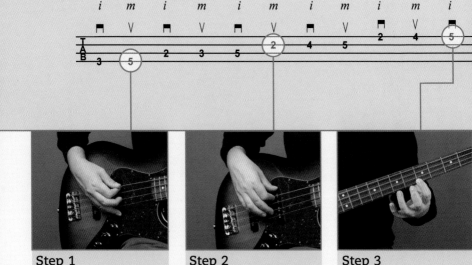

Step 1

Remember to use alternate picking when practicing this scale pickstyle. You should up-pick on the fourth string for the second note of the scale.

Step 2

Alternate picking technique should also be used when playing fingerstyle. Here, the jump from the third to the second string is illustrated (D to E): the first finger (i) is at rest on the fourth string while the second (m) plays the second string.

Step 3

After you've played the second note on the first string with your third finger (fourth fret), move your whole hand up the neck, leading with your first finger which plays the next note on the fifth fret.

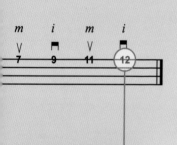

Step 4

Here you can see the fingers still in position after playing the final three notes, with the pinky fretting the high G on the twelfth fret. Keeping your fingers on the fretboard in this way will make descending the scale much easier.

Understanding basics

An interval in music describes the distance between two notes. All intervals are referenced in relation to the major scale, where all of the intervals are major or perfect. So, when the scale is written numerically (1–2–3–4–5–6–7–8) there are no flat or sharp signs in the formula. For instance, a minor third would be written as ♭3, but since the third in the scale is major, it is written simply as a number. Thinking of scales in this way makes it much easier to transpose them to different keys. Both major and minor chords, plus the all-important perfect cadence (a musical full-stop), can be constructed using the major scale. Quite simply, it's one of the most important note resources for a musician—it is truly the mother of all scales!

Listen up!

Interval checker

T1 = root or tonic
2 = major second
3 = major third
4 = perfect fourth
5 = perfect fifth
6 = major sixth
7 = major seventh

Roots and fifths

With nothing more than a chord sequence for inspiration, the idea of creating basslines on the fly might seem like an impossible call. But armed with a few essential tips and tools, you'll be able to create spontaneous accompaniments to any chord progression.

You can use any finger to fret the higher note. Here, you can see the third finger hovering above the seventh fret while the open string is played.

Understanding the perfect fifth

Basslines are generally constructed from the notes contained within the chords of a sequence. Sometimes, extra notes are added to create more melodic lines; sometimes just the chord notes are used. Before we delve into more involved note choices, it's essential that you understand the root and fifth approach—a simple technique for creating basslines.

The perfect fifth is a "safe" interval; it is neither major nor minor and so it can be applied to most chord types. As its name implies, the perfect fifth interval is five letter names above its root, i.e. the fifth of C is G, the fifth of A is E (the first letter must be counted). The Cycle of Fifths diagram on page 67 will help you find the fifth of any note. Sometimes, the note needs to be sharpened or flattened to preserve the 3½-tone (7 frets) distance required to create a perfect fifth.

Because all of these root to fifth examples start with an open string, the fretted note (fifth) is played with the second finger.

Top tip

Memorize the moveable shapes for ascending and descending perfect fifths, then you won't have to think when you need one in a hurry—the answer will be under your fingers!

Example 1

Playing the perfect fifth interval ascending on the same string illustrates exactly how big the interval is. Although these open string patterns can only be applied in limited harmonic scenarios, they are still worth memorizing.

Example 2

By moving the fifth onto an adjacent string the second note appears "closer." This is the most useful shape when playing ascending root to fifth basslines.

Continued over the page >>>

Fret the lower note of this moveable shape with your first finger. Allow your third finger to hover above the third fret while you're playing the first note, as illustrated.

Example 3

Converting the previous open string pattern to two fretted notes provides a completely moveable shape that can be applied anywhere on the neck, starting on any note.

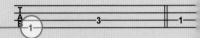

Practice the Paganini technique (see the glossary on page 250) using each of your four fretting-hand fingers. Here, you can see the first finger fretting the first note of the first bar. When it returns to upright position, it will automatically be fretting the lower note, as in the photo to your right.

Example 4

To descend from the root to the fifth, play on the adjacent lower string on the same fret as the root. These are easier to play when fretting with one finger. Use the Paganini technique (i.e. rolling one finger across the strings) that we explored back in Lesson 8 (page 41).

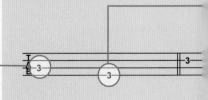

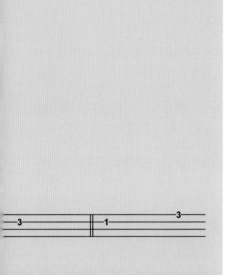

The history of the root and fifth

Before the electric bass or double bass took the jazz world by storm, the tuba was the bass instrument in marching and "trad" jazz bands. Since the tuba is not an agile instrument, the basslines consisted mainly of roots and fifths—the most effective way to support a chord sequence with the minimum number of notes. The root and fifth approach is predominant in Latin and country, but it's such an effective technique that it can be found in all genres, from classical music to heavy metal.

Listen up!

Cycle of fifths

This handy diagram will help you to find the fifth of any chord. Read it clockwise to find the perfect fifth of any note (counter-clockwise spells perfect fourths). Note that some notes have two names; this is known as an enharmonic spelling (see page 77).

14 *Country workout*

Like jazz, country is an exclusive product of the USA. Unlike jazz, it is hugely popular in the States, which makes it one of the biggest-selling styles of music in the world. Whether you're a country fan or not, don't skip this chapter. Not only is the country workout an invaluable resource for applying your root and fifth technique, you'll discover that country music is great fun to play and very addictive.

Keeping time

Country music is generally played in "cut time" (2/2 as opposed to 4/4). These two time signatures are identical: 2 half-note beats per bar and 4 quarter-note beats per bar add up to the same number of notes. However, it's the subtle differences in groove and tempo that make these two time

Johnny Cash is considered to be one of the most influential American country singer-songwriters of the twentieth century.

Add it to your downloads!

signatures sound very different. For a start, 2/2 (or "cut time") implies two bass notes per bar and—yes, you've guessed it pardners—the root and fifth will do nicely!

The role of the bass in country

Because most country is played in "cut time" with the bass falling on beats one and two, it's the bass player's job to stick to a simple alternating root and fifth bassline. The bass is the one constant throughout the arrangement, and holds everything together, whether underpinning a lush harmony or a vocal-laden chorus, or holding down a breakneck solo section in a fast western swing hoedown. It's acceptable to add other notes between the beats, but the all-important "one, two, one, two" groove must be maintained.

Top tip

Keep all notes short in country-style pieces, by muting them. This really allows the drum part to "breathe" by creating space for the snare drum.

Chet Atkins
The Amazing Chet Atkins
Released in 1955 and featuring the Anita Kerr Singers, this epitomizes the Nashville sound and captures Chet Atkins at his best.

Johnny Cash
At Folsom Prison
Cash performed in many prisons throughout his career. This recording includes the "Man in Black," performed at the Californian prison in 1968.

Oh Brother, Where Art Thou?
Film Soundtrack
The soundtrack for the 2000 Coen brothers' movie reunited Americans with their musical heritage. It features artists such as Alison Krauss and Gillian Welch alongside original bluegrass stars like Ralph Stanley.

The Eagles
Hotel California
Released in 1976, this "all winner, no filler" classic captures the hedonistic country rockers at the very peak of their game.

Continued over the page >>>

Example 1: This tune is in the style of a classic western swing groove; so all eighth notes have a swing feel, as they would in blues or jazz. Although country basslines rarely include eighth notes, accomplished players would still imply the swing feel in the subtle nuances of their performance.

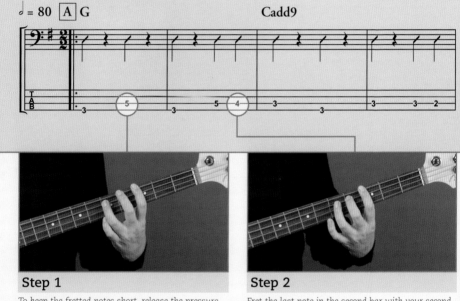

Step 1

To keep the fretted notes short, release the pressure of your finger without taking it off the strings. Here, the second note is being played with the third finger while the first mutes the low G.

Step 2

Fret the last note in the second bar with your second finger. Slide the finger down the string and use it to fret the following note too.

On the CD Tracks 25–26

Listen up!

Fingerstyle for country!
This piece should be played fingerstyle
with alternating fingers throughout.
Country music originally relied on the
double bass, so an organic, natural
sound works best. This can only be
achieved effectively with the fingers.

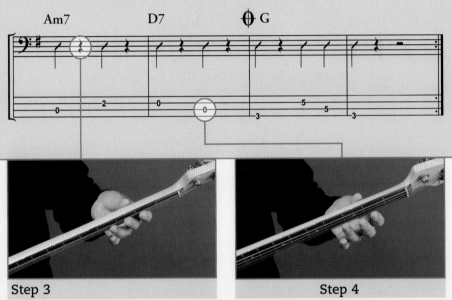

Step 3

Remember that open strings should be damped with
the fretting hand fingers laying flat across the strings
as illustrated.

Step 4

When consecutive open strings are played, it's
essential that you prevent them from ringing into
each other with efficient muting. Here, the fingers
hover flat across the second and third fret, waiting to
damp the third string.

Continued over the page >>>

Listen up!

Chord symbols

Chord symbols have been placed above the stave for two reasons: 1) you may have a guitar-playing mate who'd like to join in; 2) it allows you to analyze the note choices with reference to the harmony. Notice that sometimes an extra note is added on the fourth beat; this is usually a passing note (i.e. not necessarily a chord note) that eases the harmony into a chord change (like at the end of bar two).

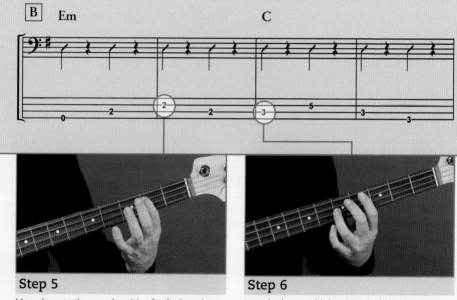

Step 5

Move down to the second position for the B section. Here you can see the first finger applying the Paganini technique to the notes in the second bar.

Step 6

Move back up to third position in this bar, using your first finger for C. This leaves your third finger ready for the high G that follows.

On the CD Tracks 25–26

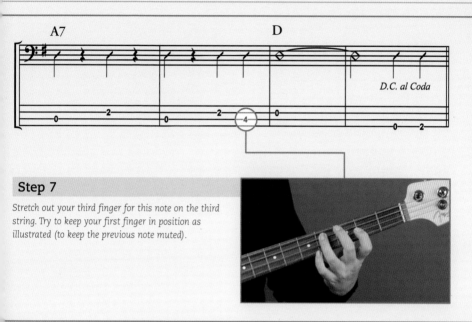

Step 7

Stretch out your third finger for this note on the third string. Try to keep your first finger in position as illustrated (to keep the previous note muted).

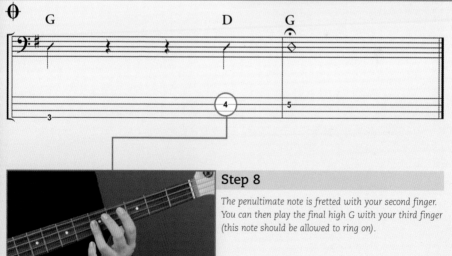

Step 8

The penultimate note is fretted with your second finger. You can then play the final high G with your third finger (this note should be allowed to ring on).

Major arpeggios

Once you've sussed how roots
and fifths work, it's easy to add
a major third to create a major
arpeggio. Learn your arpeggios
carefully—you'll have more
notes to choose from when
you're jamming with the band
or learning new songs.

*Use your first finger for the second note. Play
the seventh fret note with your fourth finger.
Here, the fourth finger plays the highest note
of an E major arpeggio with the first finger
in position.*

What is an arpeggio?

An arpeggio is simply a chord
played melodically (when notes
are played consecutively) instead
of harmonically (when all notes
are sounded simultaneously, as in
a chord or double stop). A major
arpeggio consists of three notes: a
root note, major third, and perfect
fifth. These notes can be constructed
using the major scale we studied in
Lesson 12 on pages 60–63, but it's
far better to understand how the
arpeggio is constructed as a separate
entity. If you can manage this,
you will be able to apply the notes
anywhere on the neck, in any key.

*All of these patterns are played in second
position (i.e. with the first and third fingers
only). This photo illustrates the second note
of the E major arpeggio played with the
third finger. Note the first finger already
hovering in position for the last note.*

▶▶**See also:** Arpeggio library, starting on page 216

Example 1
Major arpeggio on one string
In Lesson 12, you learned how to negotiate
the distance between the notes of a perfect
fifth when played along one string. The
same principles apply to the major arpeggio.
In this example, a major arpeggio starts
on each of the bass guitar's strings with
all three notes played on the same string.
Notice that the major third is two whole
steps (or four frets) above its root note.

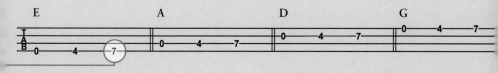

Example 2
Major arpeggio on adjacent strings (type-1)
By moving the last note of the arpeggio onto
a higher string, the shape spans far fewer
frets and is therefore easier to play.

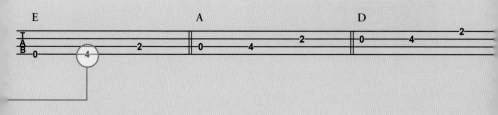

Continued over the page >>>

Another arpeggio that uses only the first and third fingers is the adjacent string type-2 pattern. Notice how the third finger is already in position above the third fret as the first finger plays the root of F major.

Example 3
Major arpeggio on adjacent strings (type-2)
Moving the third and fifth onto a higher string results in the most useful major arpeggio shape. These are the only major arpeggios that can be played with an open second note.

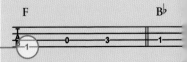

The moveable major arpeggio shape starts on the second finger and finishes on the fourth. Fret the final note of the F♯ major arpeggio with your fourth finger.

Example 4
Major arpeggio moveable shape
By shifting the previous examples up a half step, three indispensable patterns are created. These contain no open strings, so they can be moved anywhere on the neck to create a major arpeggio starting on any note.

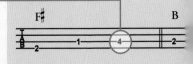

Listen up!

C = C major chord

You'll notice that the chord symbols used in these examples don't have a "maj" abbreviation. That's because a capital letter on its own is understood to mean "major" when used as a chord symbol.

E♭

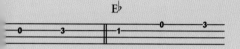

Listen up!

Enharmonic notes

We touched on enharmonic notes in Lesson 13 (page 64). This is when a note has two names, e.g. C♯ is the same as D♭. When you're spelling arpeggios out (particularly to other musicians) make sure your third is three letter names above the root and the fifth is five letter names above the root (don't forget to count the root as "1"). In other words the correct name for the major third of E is G♯ and not A♭. It's the same note on the fretboard, but an incorrect use of musical grammar that could be frowned upon!

E

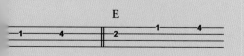

Continued over the page >>>

The first-inversion pattern is quite a tricky one. Ideally the fourth fret notes should be played with the fourth finger. If this is uncomfortable, or your pinky simply isn't strong enough yet, try using your third finger as shown in this photo.

Example 5
First inversion moveable shapes

The arpeggios in this example all have the major third as their lowest note (i.e. D♭ major starts on an F). Arpeggios or chords that have the third as their lowest note are described as being "first inversion."

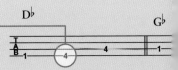

After the big stretch involved in the previous example you should find the second-inversion pattern easier. Use your first finger for the lowest notes, rolling across the fretboard using the Paganini technique (page 41), as shown here.

Example 6
Second inversion moveable shapes

The second-inversion major arpeggio has the fifth interval as its lowest note. As this shape spans three strings, there are only two patterns: one starting on the fourth string, the other on the third string.

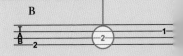

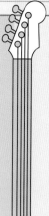

Top tip

Pick a random note. Try to imagine the major third and fifth by visualizing the moveable shape-2 pattern. This will help you to identify other intervals.

B

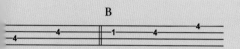

Listen up!

Arpeggio inversions

It is possible to play arpeggios that start on either the third or the fifth instead of the root; these are called inversions. Inversions contain the same notes as a root position arpeggio, just in a different order. Inversions are extremely useful for creating basslines that start on a high root note—that is: C or above on the third string.

• root position = **1–3–5**

• first inversion = **3–5–1**

• second inversion = **5–1–3**

E

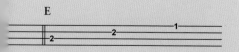

16 *The minor pentatonic scale*

The minor pentatonic scale has been responsible for some of the most iconic riffs in popular music history. It's found in every style of music but most predominantly in blues, jazz, and rock.

The history of the pentatonic

The term "pentatonic" is an amalgam of two Ancient Greek words; *pente* meaning five and *tonic*, which means tone. The term, therefore, can be applied to any five-tone (note) scale, of which there are many different varieties. The pentatonic scale predates the major scale by thousands of years: in fact, it is believed to be the first scale that mankind used to create melody, and is evident in Ancient Greek, Chinese, African, and Eastern European music. Perhaps it's the simplistic, primeval appeal of this scale that makes it particularly effective in rock music. The driving rhythms and riffs awaken in us a subconscious recollection of simpler times deep in our history. Overall, the pentatonic scale is foolproof: since it contains no semitones (half-step notes), it contains no dissonant intervals. This makes it especially useful for improvisation and riff construction.

Example 1

This is the one-octave E minor pentatonic scale in open position. The last note is the octave E, which is played once before descending. Note that the fingering used indicates that the scale should be played in second position (i.e. with the first finger on the second fret).

Step 1

Play the first fretted note with your second finger. Aim to keep your first finger in position for the following note, hovering over the second fret as shown.

▶▶**See also:** Scale library, starting on page 166

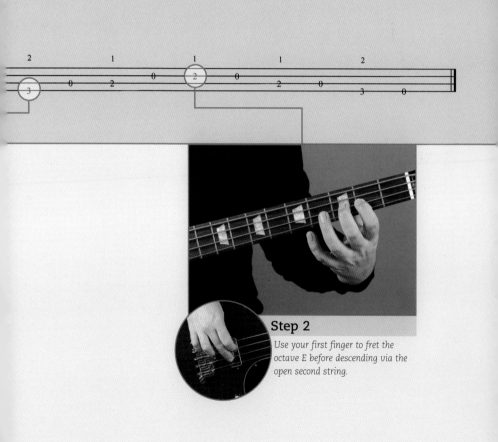

Step 2

Use your first finger to fret the octave E before descending via the open second string.

Continued over the page >>>

Example 2

This scale adds the upper octave on the first string to create a full two-octave scale. Notice that the higher notes are fretted with the first and third fingers only. Alternate picking should be used for pick and fingerstyle technique throughout.

Step 1

Play the second fret on the first string with your first finger. Note the third finger already hovering above the fourth fret.

Listen up!

Minor pentatonic scale construction

W = whole step (2 frets or tone)

W+H = whole + half step (3 frets or minor third)

$$1 - {}^\flat 3 - 4 - 5 - {}^\flat 7 - \text{Oct}$$
$$\text{W+H} \quad \text{W} \quad \text{W} \quad \text{W+H} \quad \text{W}$$

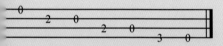

Listen up!

Interval checker

1 = root or tonic
$^\flat$3 = minor third
4 = perfect fourth
5 = perfect fifth
$^\flat$7 = minor seventh

Step 2

The quick jump to the seventh fret is executed with your first finger. Try to keep the finger in contact with the first string (without fretting) as you move up the neck.

Continued over the page >>>

Example 3

By shifting the scale up a half step, the moveable shape-1 (there are ultimately five shapes for every scale) minor pentatonic scale is created. Use the fingering indicated and alternate pick and fingerstyle technique. Remember that this is a moveable shape (playing it as shown creates the F minor pentatonic), so if you find it too much of a stretch to play in this position, simply move the shape higher up the neck.

Step 1

Keep your left hand in the first position for this scale, playing the second note of the scale with your fourth finger.

Top tip

Sing each note of the scale before playing it on your bass. This will accelerate the sensitivity of your ear to different sounds and pitches.

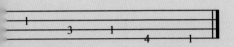

Step 2

Once you're off the fourth string, you can play all the remaining notes with your first and third fingers. This picture shows the first note played with the first finger while the third finger hovers above the third fret.

Listen up!

Left-hand positions
These are numbered according to which fret the first finger is on. So the "third position" means that your first finger plays notes on the third fret.

Moveable shapes
Moveable shapes are lifesavers when you're confronted with strange keys or awkward chord progressions: you'll be able to handle any harmony the band throws at you. For example, turn an F sharp major riff into an A flat major riff by moving your hand up two positions (two frets). Pretty handy, isn't it?

Blues in E

The 12-bar blues is the first chord sequence that most guitarists and bass players learn—it's the staple fare at jam sessions around the globe. Traditionally found in blues arrangements, the chord sequence has been "borrowed" and used in just about every other genre from jazz to pop. In fact, this chord sequence is so deeply embedded in the psyche of contemporary music that you cannot afford to ignore it!

Get practicing!

Musicians prefer to think of chord progressions in relation to the scale steps of the major scale. As a result, it's very easy to instantly transpose a sequence to another key (any professional musician worth their salt should be able to do this on the fly). On a gig it's not uncommon for the bandleader to shout out a key for a standard chord sequence immediately before counting the tune in (for example, "blues in E♭" or "rhythm changes in C"). There's no time to think in these situations, you've just got to know your stuff and play the right note on that first downbeat or you won't get booked again. So get practicing!

Example 1

Here is the 12-bar blues in its most widely used and simplest form. Chord symbols have been given in the key of E major; the roman numerals above indicate the root movement of the sequence so that it may be applied to other keys easily.

$$\text{I7}$$
𝄢 $\frac{4}{4}$ E7 / / / | / / / / | / / / / | / / / / |

⁵ IV7 I7
𝄢 A7 / / / | / / / / | E7 / / / | / / / / |

⁹ V7 IV7 I7 V7
𝄢 B7 / / / | A7 / / / | E7 / / / | / / B7 / ‖

Listen up!

Roman numeral systems

Musicians use the roman numeral system to describe chord sequences, making it easier to transpose progressions to other keys. Transposing is usually for the benefit of a singer, or horns (sax/trumpet), or sometimes just because it sounds better.

I7 = Dominant seventh on root

IV7 = Dominant seventh on fourth step (count 5 frets up from your root note)

V7 = Dominant seventh on fifth step (count 7 frets up from your root note)

Continued over the page >>>

Example 2

This is a 12-bar blues in E with a one bar repeated bass riff that moves to the A7 chord in the fifth bar. "Blues shuffle" next to the tempo indication means that the eighth notes should be played with swing feel. Listen to the full mix on the CD before and you should have no problems interpreting the shuffle groove—it's an instantly recognizable rhythm that you will have heard on many famous recordings. The E7/B chord in the first and second time bars is a chord inversion. Whenever you see an inversion symbol play the right-hand note instead of the root note of the chord. The B is the fifth of the E7 chord so technically this is a second inversion E7.

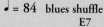

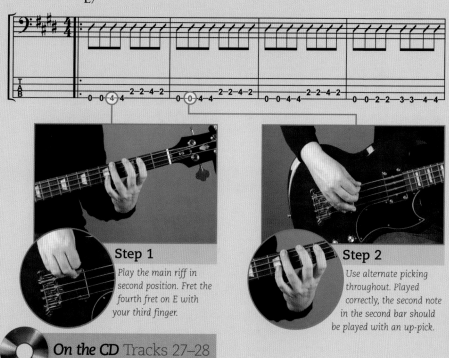

Step 1

Play the main riff in second position. Fret the fourth fret on E with your third finger.

Step 2

Use alternate picking throughout. Played correctly, the second note in the second bar should be played with an up-pick.

On the CD Tracks 27–28

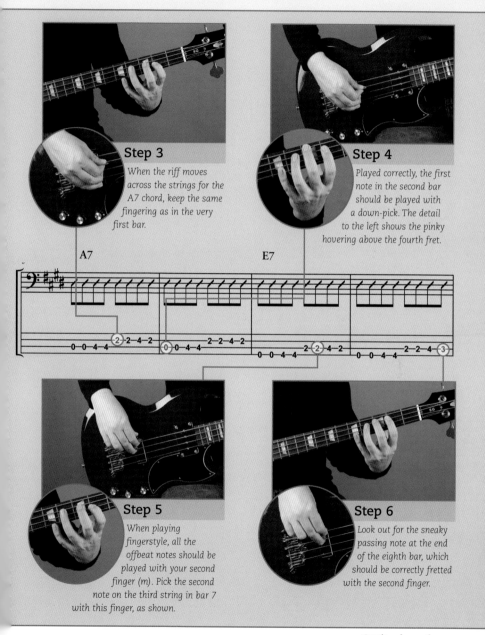

Step 3

When the riff moves across the strings for the A7 chord, keep the same fingering as in the very first bar.

Step 4

Played correctly, the first note in the second bar should be played with a down-pick. The detail to the left shows the pinky hovering above the fourth fret.

Step 5

When playing fingerstyle, all the offbeat notes should be played with your second finger (m). Pick the second note on the third string in bar 7 with this finger, as shown.

Step 6

Look out for the sneaky passing note at the end of the eighth bar, which should be correctly fretted with the second finger.

Continued over the page >>>

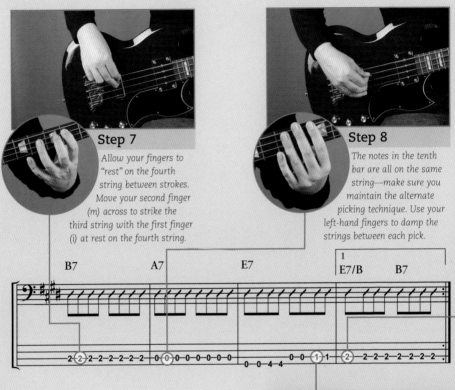

Step 7

Allow your fingers to "rest" on the fourth string between strokes. Move your second finger (m) across to strike the third string with the first finger (i) at rest on the fourth string.

Step 8

The notes in the tenth bar are all on the same string—make sure you maintain the alternate picking technique. Use your left-hand fingers to damp the strings between each pick.

B7   A7   E7   E7/B   B7

Top tip

Because this bassline uses a continuous eighth note pattern, practice the E7 and A7 riffs at a slower tempo before you attempt to play along to the CD.

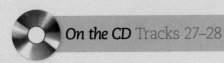

On the CD Tracks 27–28

Step 9

Grab the first fret note on the third string with your first finger. Here you can see the last pair of notes in the eleventh bar played with the first finger.

Step 10

Use your first finger for the first note in both the first and second time bars. This returns your fingers to second position.

Step 11

Play the penultimate note with your first finger. As soon as you've played the preceding note on the third string, move your first finger into position. Don't forget that the tempo is slowing at this point so there's no need to panic!

Listen up!

Slowing things down

Sometimes, usually at the end of a piece, the instruction "rit" (ritardando) or "rall" (rallentando) is added above or below the stave. This indicates that the tempo should be pulled back, often to make endings more dramatic. In a gig situation this would be directed by one band member who would give visual cues to other musicians.

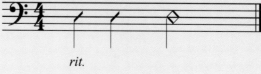

The natural minor scale

The tone of the natural minor is more ambiguous and complex than major tonality. Make sure you get to grips with the major scale (Lesson 12; page 60) before you grapple with this lesson and you will be able to detect the slight nuances of sound, pitch, and mood.

Understanding basics

There isn't one definitive minor scale to mirror the major; there are in fact four principal minor scales: natural minor, Dorian mode, harmonic, and melodic minor. Each minor key has a "relative" major key cousin a minor third (three frets) above. So the relative major key of A minor is C major and vice versa. The natural minor scale (also known as the Aeolian mode) uses exactly the same notes as its relative major cousin, making it the obvious minor scale to start with.

Example 1

This one-octave E natural minor shape uses the same three-note pattern on the fourth and third strings. The scale should be played in first position both ascending and descending.

Step 1

Because this scale starts with an open string, make sure your fingers are hovering in first position before you play the first note.

▸▸**See also:** Scale library, starting on page 166

Listen up!

Finding the relative minor

To find the relative minor of any major key, just count down three frets (minor third) from your major key root note. Using this system, it's easy to calculate that E minor is the relative minor of G major. So if we take the G major scale notes (G–A–B–C–D–E–F♯–G) but start the scale on the E (E–F♯–G–A–B–C–D–E), a very different sound is produced. This new scale has a minor third, minor sixth, and minor seventh. The minor third establishes the minor tonality of the scale while the minor sixth and seventh heighten the modal, "folksy" quality.

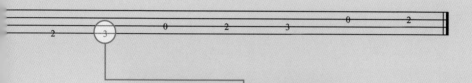

Step 2

Try to keep your fingers in position when adding higher notes on the same string. This photo illustrates the third note on the third string fretted with the third finger but with the second finger still fretting the previous note.

Continued over the page >>>

Example 2

By adding extra notes on the first string, a full two-octave pattern can be achieved for the E natural minor. As with the one-octave shape, start in first position, shifting up the neck on the first string using the fingering indicated.

Step 1

The full two-octave scale incorporates the F♯ on the second string which you should play with your fourth finger, as shown.

Step 2

While playing the open first string, move your hand up to first position for the next three notes, as shown.

Listen up!

Scale construction

W = whole step (2 frets or tone)

W+H = whole + half step (3 frets or minor third)

$$1 - 2 - \flat 3 - 4 - 5 - \flat 6 - \flat 7 - \text{Oct}$$
$$ W \quad H \quad W \quad W \quad H \quad W \quad W$$

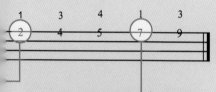

Step 3

To shift to seventh position, slide your first finger up the string. Here you can see the seventh fret on the first string played with the first finger (note the third finger is hovering above the ninth fret).

Listen up!

Interval checker

1 = root or tonic
2 = major second
$\flat 3$ = minor third
4 = perfect fourth
5 = perfect fifth
$\flat 6$ = minor sixth
$\flat 7$ = minor seventh

Continued over the page >>>

Example 3

Shift the original pattern up a minor third (three frets) and add the extra notes on the first string, and you will create a shape-1 pattern for G natural minor. This is a moveable shape and can be played anywhere on the neck. If you find third position difficult to play in, simply move the shape up the neck to a higher position.

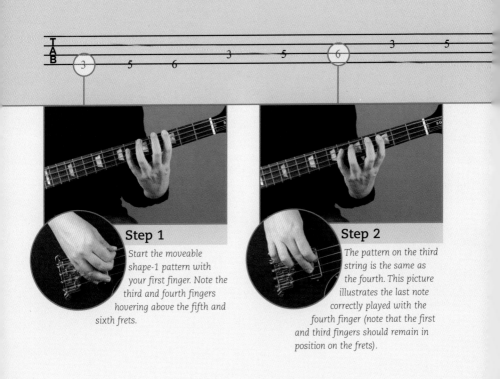

Step 1

Start the moveable shape-1 pattern with your first finger. Note the third and fourth fingers hovering above the fifth and sixth frets.

Step 2

The pattern on the third string is the same as the fourth. This picture illustrates the last note correctly played with the fourth finger (note that the first and third fingers should remain in position on the frets).

Top tip

Alternate picking/fingerstyle
technique. Only the ascending
scale is shown, but practice both
ascending and descending without
repeating the top note.

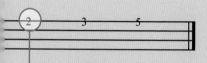

Step 3

*Jump to second position
for the notes on the top
string. Here you can
see the fourth fret on
the first string played with
the first finger while the second
and fourth fingers hover over their
respective frets. Use the same
position shift when descending.*

Listen up!

Improvisation

As soon as you can play a scale
or arpeggio pattern up and down
in your sleep, it's time to have
some fun with it. Play the notes
of the scale (or arpeggio) in any
order you like, and to any rhythm.
Improvisers may seem to be
plucking music out of thin air, but
in reality they're accessing a huge
(or not so huge) memorized library
of scales, arpeggios, and licks
(mini-melodies). Improvising with
shapes and patterns like this will
make you a more impressive and
spontaneous bassist in a session
or rehearsal.

Minor arpeggios

If you don't know your arpeggios, how to play or apply them, you'll severely limit your options when the time comes to create your own basslines.

Major and minor variations

Just like the major arpeggios you should now be familiar with (take a sneaky peak at Lesson 15 on page 74 if you need to refresh your memory), the minor arpeggio also consists of three notes: a root, minor third, and perfect fifth. Look back to the previous lesson and you'll notice that these intervals are the same as the first, third, and fifth steps of the natural minor scale. That is why musicians practice scales and arpeggios together, playing the scale followed by the related arpeggio or vice versa. It ensures the ability to instantly (and fluently) play a chord tone or a "color" tone. The chord tones will happily work with their related chords; the "color" tones will react against the harmony with varying degrees of dissonance. Being able to manipulate this dissonance skillfully is what being a good musician is all about.

Use your first finger on the third fret. Then, play the seventh fret with your fourth finger. You will need to move your hand up the neck to reach the highest note of the E minor arpeggio with the fourth finger.

Play these patterns in second position (i.e. using the second and third fingers). Here, the second finger plays the minor third of the E minor arpeggio (with the second finger hovering above the second fret).

▶▶**See also:** Arpeggio library, starting on page 216

Example 1
Minor arpeggio on one string
Compare this with the major
arpeggios in example 1 on page
75: the minor third is only one and
a half steps (three frets) above its
root note. The distance between
the minor third and the fifth is
consequently increased to two
whole steps so the fifth remains
on the seventh fret.

Top tip
Remember that examples 4, 5, and 6
(pages 101–103) are moveable shapes
and can be played in different positions
on the neck.

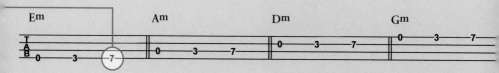

Example 2
**Minor arpeggio on adjacent
strings (type-1)**
Move the third note (fifth) onto
an adjacent string and a more
practical shape is achieved. As
these patterns span two strings,
only three shapes are formed.

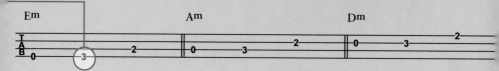

Continued over the page >>>

This arpeggio shape uses only the first and third fingers. As shown, play the root of F♯ minor with your first finger. Notice that the third finger is already in position above the fourth fret even though the following note is an open string.

Example 3
Minor arpeggio on adjacent strings (type-2)
You must move the root up a whole step before the second note (minor third) can be moved to a higher string. This pattern has a four-fret span even when played open, so it's less practical than example 1.

The moveable minor arpeggio shape uses the fourth finger for the second note. Here, the fourth finger frets the sixth fret while the third finger is hovering above the fourth fret of the third string.

Example 4
Minor arpeggio moveable shape
This pattern is the type-1 shape minor arpeggio but with its root on the third fret. By changing the root to a fretted note, a pattern that can be played anywhere on the neck is created.

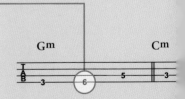

Listen up!

Chord symbols
All the chord symbols in these examples use the "m" abbreviation to indicate that they are minor. Although the small "m" is perfectly adequate, you may also see "min" used.

Cm = C minor chord

Enharmonic notes
Don't forget that an enharmonic faux pas is likely to be frowned upon by other musicians so make sure you're using the correct letters to spell your arpeggios/chords. Don't forget a minor third is three letter names above the root and a fifth is five letter names above the root (the root is "1"). Avoid mixing flat letters with sharp letters—this shouldn't happen if you're spelling a chord correctly.

Arpeggio inversion formulae

root position = 1–$\flat$3–5

first inversion = $\flat$3–5–1

second inversion = 5–1–$\flat$3

Em

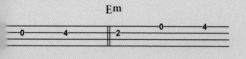

Fm

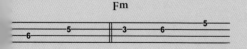

Continued over the page >>>

The first-inversion shape is fairly easy but involves using the Paganini technique (see the glossary on page 250) for the notes on the second and third strings, as shown.

Example 5
First inversion moveable shapes
Because this moveable pattern spans three strings, only two shapes can be generated.

Em

As in the previous example, the second inversion involves rolling your finger across two adjacent strings. Here, you can see the second finger applying the technique to the two lowest notes.

Example 6
Second inversion moveable shapes
As in the previous example, there are only two possible patterns because three strings are required to play the shape.

Gm

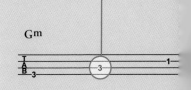

Top tip

In lesson 15 you learned about inversions (where the root is no longer the lowest note). Turn back to page 74 to refresh your memory, before you attempt these patterns.

Am

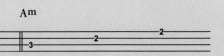

Listen up!

Practice

It's a truism that "practice makes perfect," but it's not necessarily true. Practice can actually make things worse, from reinforcing bad habits to giving you repetitive strain or other injuries (see page 17). You should remain conscientious at all stages. Is your playing even? Is your rhythm solid? Are your notes clear? Are there any unnecessary movements in your technique? Are you playing the right note? Is your instrument in tune? A great way to get another perspective on your playing is to record yourself, or even film yourself—the results can be a (somewhat scary) revelation!

Fm

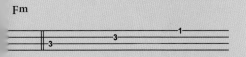

20 *Minor etude*

There's no disputing the fact that minor melodies sound sadder than major ones. Scales may be just a series of notes, but each collection of notes conjures up a completely different emotion, as you will soon find out.

Once more with feeling

The major scale sounds settled, happy, jaunty, and nonchalant while the minor yearns for that far away place that you'll never visit—it's sad, reflective, and introspective. Composers have manipulated these qualities for centuries. Musicians too have their part to play in intensifying or neutralizing the major or minor quality of a tune. For example, by playing only roots, fifths, and octaves, a bassline can prevent a major chord sequence from sounding too "happy." Similarly, omitting the minor third can help to neutralize the dark, melancholic quality of a minor tune.

Example 1
This etude (a fancy name for a short study piece) is a solo bass arrangement that makes good use of the natural minor scale's color tones. The darkest color tone in the scale is the minor sixth, followed by the minor seventh, major second, and perfect fourth.

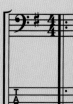

Step 1

Fret the pairs of high notes with the first and third fingers. This photo illustrates the fourteenth fret being played with the third finger and the first finger already in position for the following note.

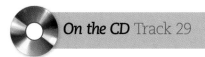

On the CD Track 29

Top tip

It's much easier to learn a new piece
if you learn it in sections. Move on
to bars 3 and 4 only when you're
comfortable with the first two bars.

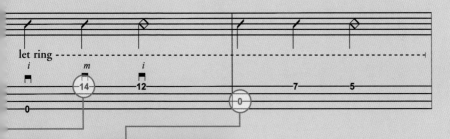

let ring

Step 2

*If you're playing fingerstyle,
take care not to rest your
thumb on the fourth string or
this note won't ring. Here you
can see the thumb correctly resting
on the thumb rest.*

Continued over the page >>>

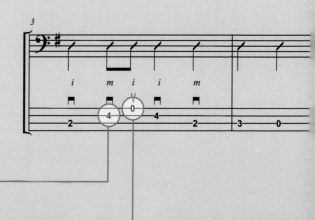

Step 3

You'll only need your first and third fingers in the third bar. This photo illustrates how the second note should be played with the third finger. The first finger should remain over the second fret for the return to the low B.

Step 4

When you're playing fingerstyle it's quite acceptable to play economy strokes by dragging one finger across the strings to play two notes. Here the first finger is about to play both the first and second strings.

On the CD Track 29

The brooding solo

It's rare that a bass player is required to play unaccompanied. Nevertheless, most bass players have at least a couple of party pieces up their sleeve. It's refreshing to play melodically; all too frequently the bassist is relegated to playing repetitive lines. The late Jaco Pastorius proved that the bass solo could be a thing of great beauty with "Portrait of Tracy," a bass solo featured on his same-titled debut album in 1976. Pastorius is one of the most highly regarded and influential electric bass players in the instrument's history. If you've never heard this man's work, you owe it to yourself to check him out!

Listen up!

The wonderful world of scales
This book covers three scales: major, natural minor, and minor pentatonic (the blues scale being a variation of the latter). While these are the most commonly used, they are only the tip of the iceberg. Every scale has its own distinct personality, and a pro will know how to choose and subtly combine elements from all scales and arpeggios to create basslines that don't just skip from one chord root to another, but have a melodic life of their own and drive the music.

Listen up!

Letting ring out
"Let ring" is written above the TAB when the notes should be allowed to ring into each other. So although it's not possible to let all the notes ring in the first two bars, the idea is to allow the open string to ring for the full bar.

21 *Chord inversions*

By now you should have a good idea of what inversions are all about—both major and minor arpeggio inversions were explored in chapters 15 (pages 74–79) and 19 (pages 98–103)— but now it's time to turn your attention to chord inversions.

What is an inversion?

An inversion occurs when a note other than the root of the chord, i.e. the third or fifth, is used in the bass. It's extremely useful to be able to recognize when you can substitute the root for another chord tone, and inversions can create smoother and more interesting basslines. There are essentially two scenarios when substituting the root note for another chord tone works well: 1) when you want to apply a "pedal" bass note to a series of chords (this is when the chords change but the bass note doesn't); 2) when you want to apply a stepwise (i.e. moving in scale steps) ascending or descending bassline to a sequence.

Example 1
The chords in this example change above a constant bass note, i.e. a pedal note (see page 111). This example would work especially well in rock music, but pedal notes aren't exclusive to the genre.

♩ = 115

Step 1
Although the octave spans just two frets, many players play this common interval with the first and fourth fingers as shown.

On the CD Tracks 30–31

▶▶**See also:** Major arpeggios on page 74

Top tip

All three of these basslines can be played with a pick or with fingers. Contemporary players are expected to be fluent with both techniques.

G5   C/G

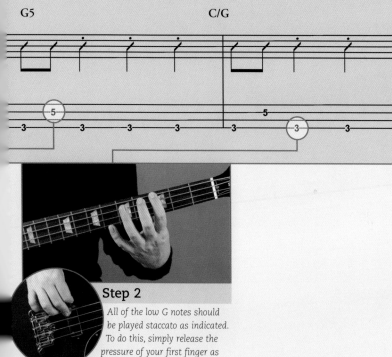

Step 2

All of the low G notes should be played staccato as indicated. To do this, simply release the pressure of your first finger as soon as you've played the note.

Continued over the page >>>

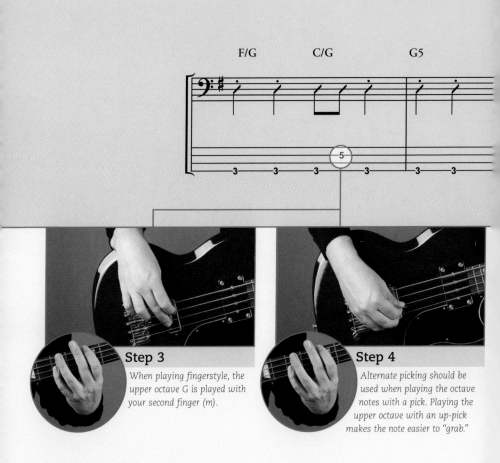

F/G   C/G   G5

Step 3

When playing fingerstyle, the upper octave G is played with your second finger (m).

Step 4

Alternate picking should be used when playing the octave notes with a pick. Playing the upper octave with an up-pick makes the note easier to "grab."

On the CD Tracks 30–31

▸▸See also: Minor arpeggios on page 98

G5

Listen up!

The "eleven" chord

You're probably wondering why a G bass note is used in the F chord inversion in Example 1 (F/G) since it doesn't occur in the triad. It's not a mistake—this is what is commonly referred to as a "slash chord." This is a triad played over an unrelated root note to create a specific chord voicing (in this case G11). Always play the bass note indicated (i.e. the letter on the right side of the slash) when confronted with slash chords or inversions.

Listen up!

Pedal notes

A pedal note is a tone sustained by one part—usually the bass—while other parts (that is: other instruments in the band, or the bass riff itself) progress without reference to it. Pedal notes (like most harmonic innovations) occurred in classical music long before popular music. They are also widely used in jazz, particularly in intros where they are used to create tension and anticipation before the tune starts.

Continued over the page >>>

Example 2
Stepwise basslines can be used ascending or descending. This example illustrates a typical descending pattern that, when repeated, creates a hypnotic, looping chord progression that might typically be used as a verse sequence.

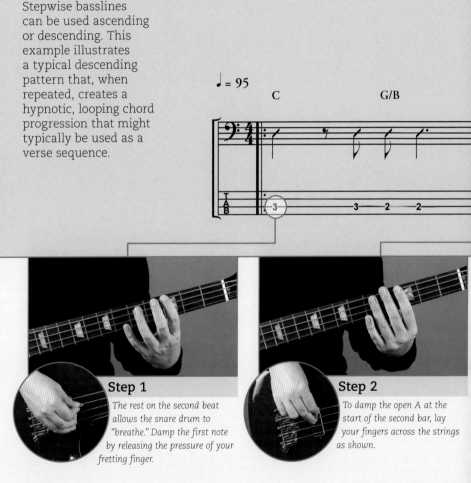

Step 1
The rest on the second beat allows the snare drum to "breathe." Damp the first note by releasing the pressure of your fretting finger.

Step 2
To damp the open A at the start of the second bar, lay your fingers across the strings as shown.

On the CD Tracks 32–33

Am C/G

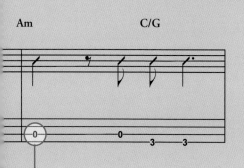

Listen up!

Power chords

Guitarists love power chords! They are prevalent in rock music but occur in many other styles too. The power chord is simply a major or minor chord with no third (i.e. it contains the root and fifth only). It's indicated by the symbol "5" after the chord. So avoid superimposing arpeggios—it's safer to stick to roots and fifths.

C5 = C power chord

Add it to your downloads!

Pedal tones

- "Just Like Paradise" (chorus) by David Lee Roth
- "Smoke On The Water" (main riff) by Deep Purple
- "Alright Now" (chorus) by Free
- "Hold Your Head Up" (main riff) by Argent

Stepwise basslines

- "Imagine" (chorus) by John Lennon
- "Let It Be" (chorus) by The Beatles
- "Babe I'm Gonna Leave You" by Led Zeppelin
- "Bohemian Rhapsody" (first guitar solo) by Queen

Continued over the page >>>

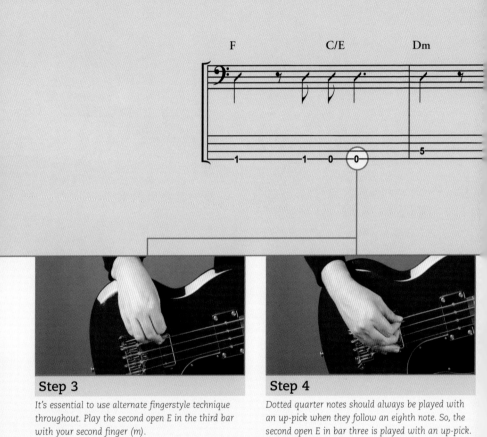

Step 3

It's essential to use alternate fingerstyle technique throughout. Play the second open E in the third bar with your second finger (m).

Step 4

Dotted quarter notes should always be played with an up-pick when they follow an eighth note. So, the second open E in bar three is played with an up-pick.

On the CD Tracks 32–33

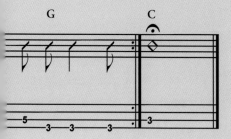

Listen up!

Don't overdo it!

The bass can be a physically demanding instrument to play and its strings are considerably heavier than those found on a guitar. Strength and dexterity are essential if you aspire to be a great bass guitarist and the only way to acquire these attributes is through regular practice. However, make sure you don't practice too much too soon. A beginner bassist's fingers will tire and blister easily and excessive practice could lead to injury. If you build up your practice gradually then your fingers will be protected by hardened skin and your hands will be less likely to tire.

Continued over the page >>>

Example 3
This last example effectively mixes both pedal notes and stepwise patterns to create a driving classic rock-style bassline.

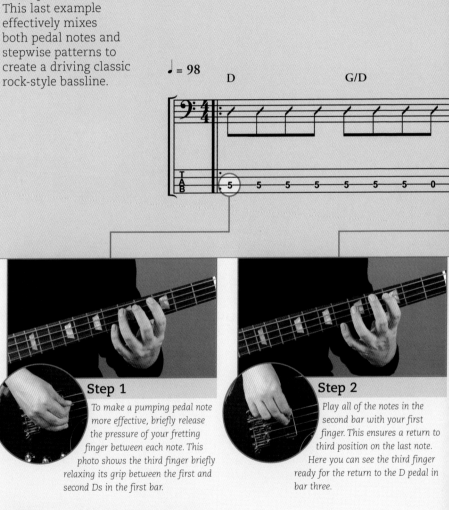

Step 1
To make a pumping pedal note more effective, briefly release the pressure of your fretting finger between each note. This photo shows the third finger briefly relaxing its grip between the first and second Ds in the first bar.

Step 2
Play all of the notes in the second bar with your first finger. This ensures a return to third position on the last note. Here you can see the third finger ready for the return to the D pedal in bar three.

On the CD Tracks 34–35

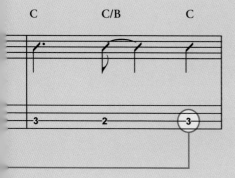

Listen up!

Tone control

You can change the tone of your playing by changing the position of your right hand. If you pick the strings close to the bridge, then your tone will be crisper and more defined. If you move your right-hand position closer to the neck, then your tone will be warmer and fuller. Some bassists even position their right hand over the neck itself!

Continued over the page >>>

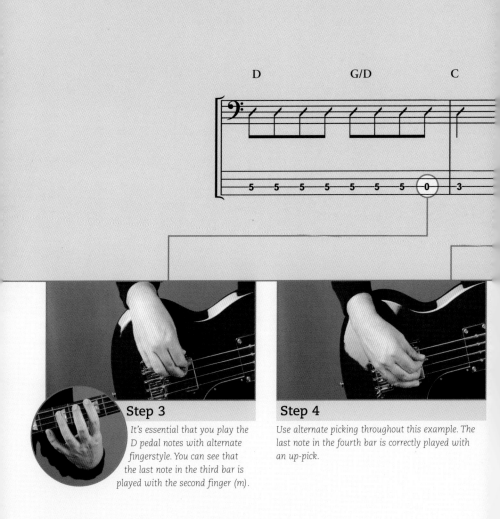

Step 3

It's essential that you play the D pedal notes with alternate fingerstyle. You can see that the last note in the third bar is played with the second finger (m).

Step 4

Use alternate picking throughout this example. The last note in the fourth bar is correctly played with an up-pick.

On the CD Tracks 34–35

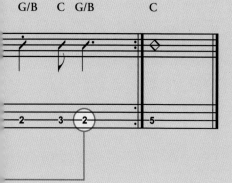

Listen up!

Tone control accessories

A typical bass guitar will have controls such as a pick-up selector and at least one tone control, sometimes marked "treble" or "bass." A bass amp will usually provide yet more tone control, but for those who hunger for more possibilities and accessories, there are various stomp boxes and effects units on the market that are capable of expanding the tonal vocabulary of your bass in a variety of subtle and not-so-subtle ways. Check out the Buyer's Guide on page 234 for the beginner must-haves.

22 Pop workout

Pop music is defined by its commercial success, which is usually short-lived and transitory. However, pop has produced some of the world's most inspirational and long-selling bands: The Beatles and The Rolling Stones.

Pop is not really a genre; it embraces only the styles that are fashionable at a particular moment in time. Its history dates back to the post-war USA of the late 1940s when 78-rpm records, and the equipment to play them on, became widely available and affordable.

One of the earliest pop charts was the Music Popularity Chart published by the American *Billboard* magazine in 1940. In 1958 the magazine published the first Hot 100 chart which runs to this day. In the UK, the first British singles chart was published by the *New Musical Express* (or *NME*) in 1952. Pop music is defined by chart

Of his time: Bill Wyman of The Rolling Stones performing at KB Hallen in Copenhagen, Denmark.

Add it to your downloads!

position more than anything else so essentially any style of music can be (and frequently has been) defined as pop, as long as it makes the charts.

The role of the bass in pop music
The first electric bass was produced by Leo Fender in 1951, just as pop was beginning to spread around the globe. It was perfect for the new and exciting sounds that were emerging. Being portable and easy to record (unlike the double bass), it could even be plugged straight into a mixing desk. It would remain the king of the bassline until its reign was challenged by the spread of electronic dance music in the 1980s. Although electronic basslines are still used today, the synthesizer never replaced the bass guitar as predicted. In fact the popularity of the instrument has never been stronger—the Fender still remains the first choice for the majority of pop artists and producers.

Generally speaking, the bass should lock with the drums and outline the harmony without being intrusive; "simple yet effective" is pop's mantra.

The Beach Boys
Pet Sounds
With its multilayered harmonies and complex arrangements, many regard this as the greatest pop album ever made.

Madonna *True Blue*
On its release in 1986, the "Queen of Pop's" third album achieved number one status in 28 countries—an unprecedented success. Madonna's career spans three decades, an extremely rare achievement in the fickle world of pop music.

Michael Jackson *Thriller*
Jackson's sixth studio album was released in 1982 and remains the biggest-selling album of any artist. Produced by the legendary Quincy Jones, it also featured diverse guest artists including Vincent Price, Paul McCartney, and guitar virtuoso Eddie Van Halen.

Continued over the page >>>

Listen up!

Double dotted notes

Double dotted notes follow the same principle as dotted notes (see page 45); they increase the duration of the note. One dot increases the note duration by half; the second dot increases it by an additional quarter of the original note. So, a double-dotted half-note would last:

2 + 1 + ½ = 3½ beats.

Example 1

This pastiche of guitar pop combines influences from The Byrds, The Beatles, Crowded House, and R.E.M.. Three playing zones are used in this arrangement: the intro is in fifth position; the "A" section open position; and the "B" section mostly in second position. This enables the majority of the notes to be played on the third and fourth strings to create a uniform tone and texture typical of pop music.

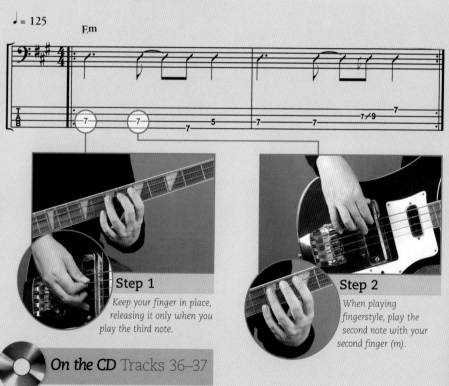

♩ = 125

F♯m

Step 1

Keep your finger in place, releasing it only when you play the third note.

Step 2

When playing fingerstyle, play the second note with your second finger (m).

On the CD Tracks 36–37

➤➤**See also:** The reggae workout on page 158

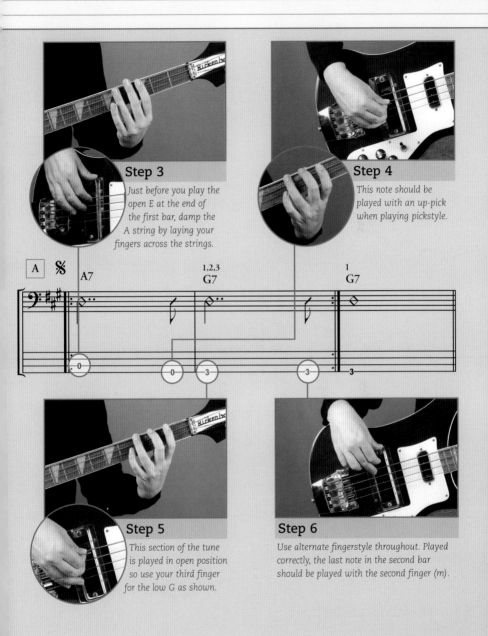

Step 3

Just before you play the open E at the end of the first bar, damp the A string by laying your fingers across the strings.

Step 4

This note should be played with an up-pick when playing pickstyle.

Step 5

This section of the tune is played in open position so use your third finger for the low G as shown.

Step 6

Use alternate fingerstyle throughout. Played correctly, the last note in the second bar should be played with the second finger (m).

Continued over the page >>>

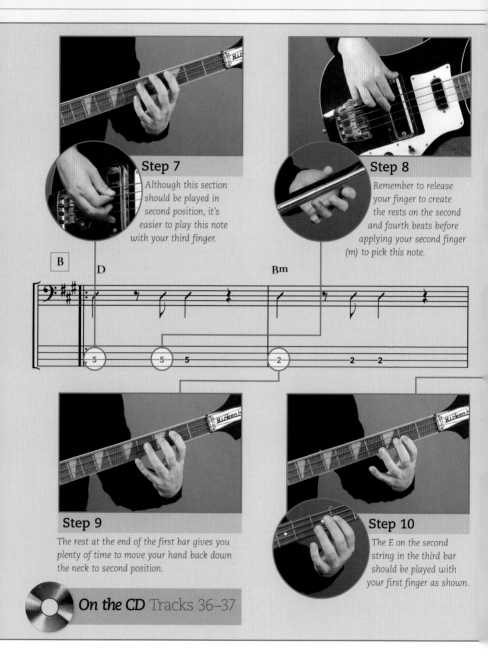

Step 7

Although this section should be played in second position, it's easier to play this note with your third finger.

Step 8

Remember to release your finger to create the rests on the second and fourth beats before applying your second finger (m) to pick this note.

Step 9

The rest at the end of the first bar gives you plenty of time to move your hand back down the neck to second position.

Step 10

The E on the second string in the third bar should be played with your first finger as shown.

On the CD Tracks 36–37

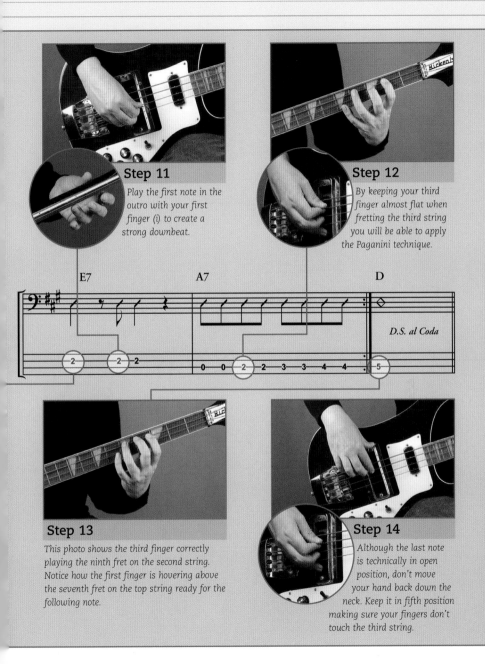

Step 11

Play the first note in the outro with your first finger (i) to create a strong downbeat.

Step 12

By keeping your third finger almost flat when fretting the third string you will be able to apply the Paganini technique.

E7   A7   D

D.S. al Coda

Step 13

This photo shows the third finger correctly playing the ninth fret on the second string. Notice how the first finger is hovering above the seventh fret on the top string ready for the following note.

Step 14

Although the last note is technically in open position, don't move your hand back down the neck. Keep it in fifth position making sure your fingers don't touch the third string.

Creating walking basslines

If I asked you to imagine a walking bassline you'd probably think of a smoky after-hours jazz club. Although walking basslines are predominantly a jazz technique, the tools used to create them are invaluable to all bass players. In fact, walking bass originated in classical music and has filtered into many other styles since.

Getting started
Walking basslines are generally improvised. Their playful tone is created by chromatic approach notes, or CAN for short. Don't let this terminology put you off— it's a wordy name for a no-brainer technique that can revolutionize your playing. Try your hand at example 1 to get the feel for walking basslines, and then turn to page 128 to discover more about the theory.

Example 1
Walking basslines involve playing a note on every beat: in 4/4 time that's four notes. A simple arpeggio consists of three notes, so you'll be one note short. So, where does the fourth note come from? You've guessed it—CAN! Ascending CANs are used here with arpeggio notes to create a smooth walking line.

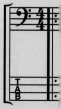

Step 1
Start in the second position using your second finger for the first note. Your first finger should be hovering above the second fret ready to hit the next note.

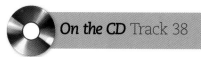

On the CD Track 38

Top tip

The best way to learn a new technique is to begin at once. Grab songbooks, chord charts, Jazz Fake Books (see page 250), and your metronome, and get walkin'!

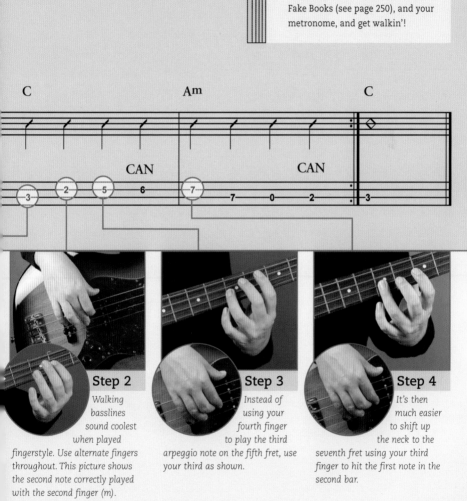

Step 2

Walking basslines sound coolest when played fingerstyle. Use alternate fingers throughout. This picture shows the second note correctly played with the second finger (m).

Step 3

Instead of using your fourth finger to play the third arpeggio note on the fifth fret, use your third as shown.

Step 4

It's then much easier to shift up the neck to the seventh fret using your third finger to hit the first note in the second bar.

Continued over the page >>>

Chromatic approach notes (CAN)

The term "chromatic" is applied to any phrase that moves in semitones (half steps) as opposed to scale steps. Typical of walking basslines, a chromatic approach note (or CAN) "approaches" its target note from a half step (one fret) above or below. As a result, the note is entirely independent of the key or chord progression that it's applied to so you don't need to worry about scales. Because CANs are usually non-diatonic (i.e. not belonging to the key), they add tension which is released when the target note is played. However, the technique needs to be applied with rhythmic consideration; if you play a CAN on beats one or three where your ear expects to hear a chord tone, it will sound odd. Play CANs on beats two and four only.

Add it to your downloads!
Famous walking basslines

- "All My Loving" by The Beatles
- "Hey Joe" by The Jimi Hendrix Experience
- "Moondance" by Van Morrison
- "Freddie Freeloader" by Miles Davis
- "Yours Is No Disgrace" by Yes
- "Stray Cat Strut" by The Stray Cats
- "Hit The Road Jack" by Ray Charles

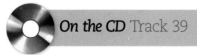

On the CD Track 39

Example 2

Ascending CANs sound smoother than descending ones. So, to create more tension, the target note should be approached from a half step above. This example is exactly the same as the previous one, except that the ascending CANs have been replaced with descending ones.

Step 1

As in the previous example, use your third finger for the third note in the first bar.

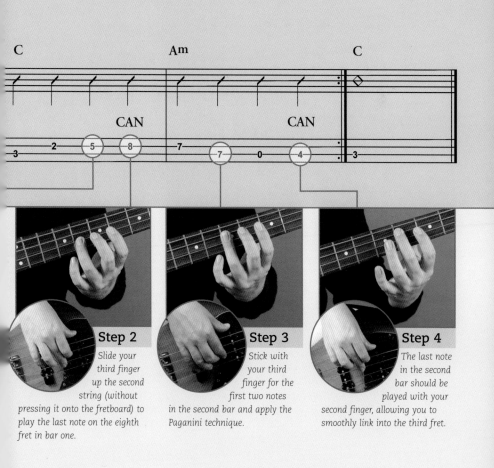

C   Am   C

CAN   CAN

3   2   5   8   7   7   0   4   3

Step 2

Slide your third finger up the second string (without pressing it onto the fretboard) to play the last note on the eighth fret in bar one.

Step 3

Stick with your third finger for the first two notes in the second bar and apply the Paganini technique.

Step 4

The last note in the second bar should be played with your second finger, allowing you to smoothly link into the third fret.

Continued over the page >>>

Example 3

When the chord progression moves in tones (whole steps) a chromatic passing note (CPN) is normally used to link the two chords smoothly. This example uses only roots and fifths with CPNs to create a cool, swinging walking line.

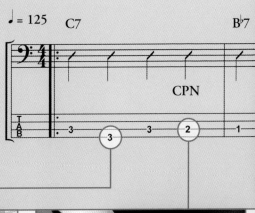

Step 1

Play both the first and second notes in the first bar with your third finger, applying the Paganini technique as shown.

Step 2

Remember that a cool, swinging sound can only really be achieved with the fingerstyle technique. Play the last note of the first bar with your second finger (m).

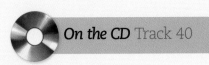

On the CD Track 40

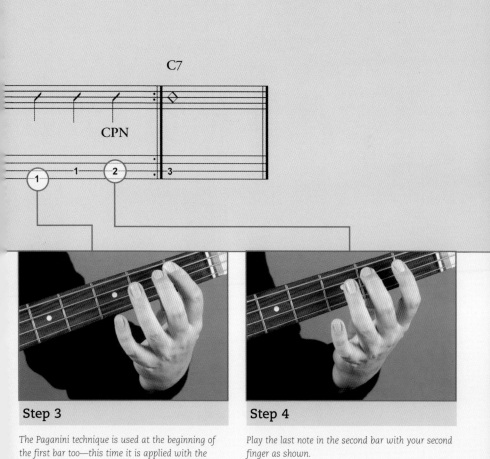

Step 3

The Paganini technique is used at the beginning of the first bar too—this time it is applied with the first finger.

Step 4

Play the last note in the second bar with your second finger as shown.

Jazz blues in B♭

When you venture into the world of jazz, you're entering that rare place where the guitar is no longer king; instead, the horn player rules.

Understanding jazz

Almost all of the jazz repertoire (including the *Great American Songbook*) is played in "horn friendly" keys. These are the flat keys: F, B♭, E♭ and A♭. The preferred keys for guitar and bass are sharp keys: D, A, and E, which can be easily negotiated with open chords or open strings. Right from the word go, you'll be starting your lines on unfamiliar notes and playing on frets you rarely use. Don't let this put you off; jazz has produced some of the most exciting and original music to date. It's challenging and fun to play, and once you get the hang of the walking bassline, you'll never be short of a gig—pop, rock, funk or otherwise.

Example 1

This demonstrates the harmonic structure of a simple jazz 12-bar blues in the key of B♭. You'll remember that the roman numerals enable you to transfer the sequence to other keys. Spot the differences by referring back to the traditional blues chord sequence (Example 1, page 86). The regular blues sequence uses just three chords; the jazz blues has six. Extra chords smooth out the sequence and make it harder to improvise over.

▶▶ **See also:** Blues in E on page 86

Add it to your downloads!

Double bass:
- Paul Chambers (Miles Davis, Kenny Burrell, John Coltrane, Wynton Kelly, et al)
- Ron Carter (Miles Davis, Wes Montgomery, George Benson, Chet Baker, Freddie Hubbard)
- Dave Holland (Miles Davis, Kenny Wheeler, Bill Frisell, plus a long career as a solo artist)

Electric bass:
- Jaco Pastorious (Pat Metheny, Weather Report, Joni Mitchell)
- Stanley Clarke (Return to Forever, Chick Corea, Pharoah Sanders)
- Anthony Jackson (Donald Fagen, Pat Metheny, Mike Stern, Billy Cobham, et al)

I7   IV7   I7   Vm7   I7

𝄢 **4/4** B♭7 / / / │ E♭7 / / / │ B♭7 / / / │ Fm7 / B♭7 / │

IV7   I7   VI7

𝄢 E♭7 / / / │ / / / / │ B♭7 / / / │ G7 / / / │

V7   IV7   I7   VI7   IIm7   V7

𝄢 Cm7 / / / │ F7 / / / │ B♭7 / G7 / │ Cm7 / F7 / ‖

Continued over the page >>>

Example 2

Despite the fact that this blues is in the bass-unfriendly key of B♭, it can be played entirely in first position and even uses a few open strings, which makes life a lot easier! The whole bassline consists of nothing more than three-note arpeggios and chromatic approach or "passing" notes (see page 128). In bars nine and ten, a well used chromatically ascending line outlines the IIm7–V7 chord change; an extremely common progression in jazz. A one-bar IIm7-V7 (Fm7-B♭7) also occurs in the fourth bar (in the key of E♭), pushing the sequence into the E♭7 chord change.

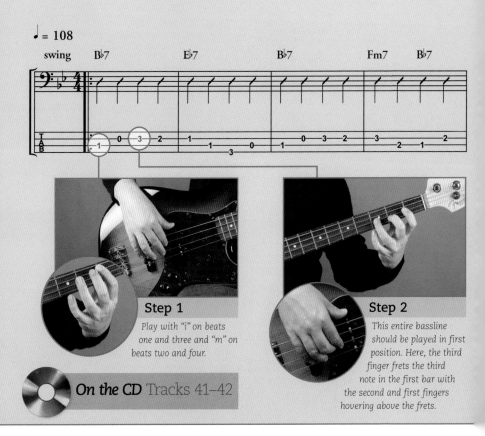

Step 1

Play with "i" on beats one and three and "m" on beats two and four.

Step 2

This entire bassline should be played in first position. Here, the third finger frets the third note in the first bar with the second and first fingers hovering above the frets.

On the CD Tracks 41–42

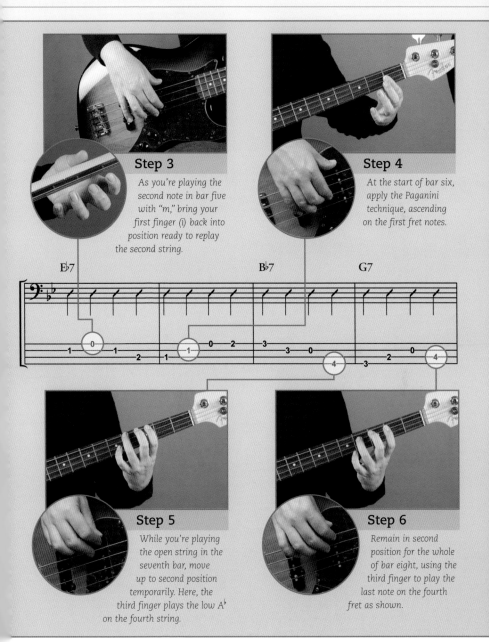

Step 3

As you're playing the second note in bar five with "m," bring your first finger (i) back into position ready to replay the second string.

Step 4

At the start of bar six, apply the Paganini technique, ascending on the first fret notes.

Step 5

While you're playing the open string in the seventh bar, move up to second position temporarily. Here, the third finger plays the low A♭ on the fourth string.

Step 6

Remain in second position for the whole of bar eight, using the third finger to play the last note on the fourth fret as shown.

Continued over the page >>>

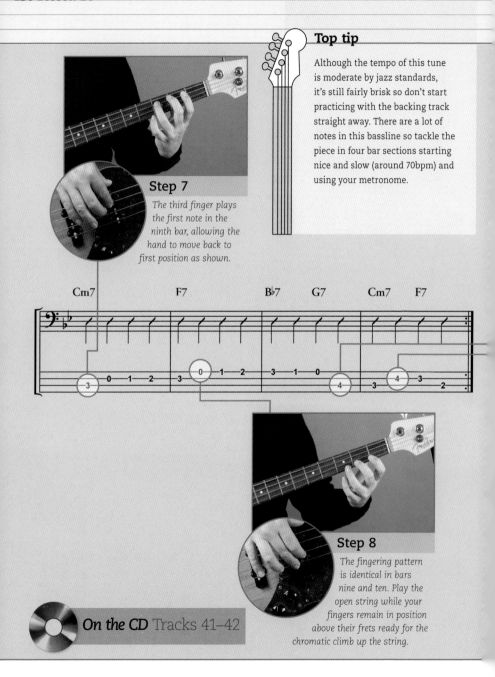

Top tip

Although the tempo of this tune is moderate by jazz standards, it's still fairly brisk so don't start practicing with the backing track straight away. There are a lot of notes in this bassline so tackle the piece in four bar sections starting nice and slow (around 70bpm) and using your metronome.

Step 7

The third finger plays the first note in the ninth bar, allowing the hand to move back to first position as shown.

Cm7   F7   Bb7   G7   Cm7   F7

Step 8

The fingering pattern is identical in bars nine and ten. Play the open string while your fingers remain in position above their frets ready for the chromatic climb up the string.

On the CD Tracks 41–42

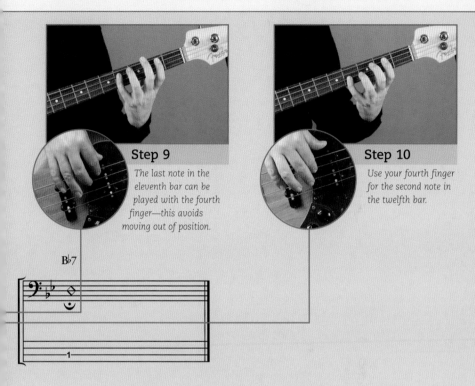

Step 9

The last note in the eleventh bar can be played with the fourth finger—this avoids moving out of position.

Step 10

Use your fourth finger for the second note in the twelfth bar.

B♭7

Listen up!

The turnaround

The function of a turnaround is to push the harmony back to the start of the song. It usually occurs in the last two bars of a sequence, most commonly consisting of a I–VI–II–V root movement, as shown below. With only two beats on each chord, the best way to negotiate the sequence is to play the root notes on beats one and three with CANs on beats two and four (i.e. how the sequence is negotiated in the last two bars of example 2).

I7	VI7	IIm7	V7
B♭7	G7	Cm7	F7

Sixteenth-note rhythms

As you already know, an eighth note is half a beat long; to play it correctly involves dividing the beat into two. Sixteenth-note rhythms up the ante by dividing the beat into four (4 x sixteenth notes = 1 beat).

Keeping time

The traditional method for counting sixteenth notes is to add "e" before the "+" and "er" after it. So the count is "one-e-and-er, two-e-and-er," which rolls off the tongue better than it reads! Accurate counting is essential, particularly when tackling syncopated sixteenth patterns—that's when the "e" and "er" notes are played individually. Generally speaking, you'll only find sixteenth-note basslines in slow to mid tempo grooves. For this type of groove the drummer often plays a sixteenth-note pattern on the hi-hat. If this sounds complicated, don't panic: with time and regular practice, you'll be able to recognize common sixteenth-note rhythms and play them without even thinking.

Example 1

Since the first note in a group of sixteenths falls on the beat and the third sixteenth falls in the same place as an offbeat eighth note (i.e. on the "+"), this leaves only the second and fourth sixteenth. In this example, the second sixteenth note (or "e") is highlighted in each bar on the second beat.

Listen up!

Accents
Notes that should be accented (by picking harder) are indicated by a right-facing chevron. These are frequently placed on weak beats to highlight a syncopated rhythm.

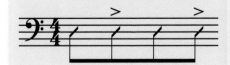

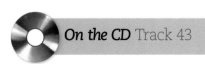

On the CD Track 43

Top tip

Although each exercise is notated as a bassline, make sure you can clap the rhythm confidently first. "If you can't clap it, you can't play it!"

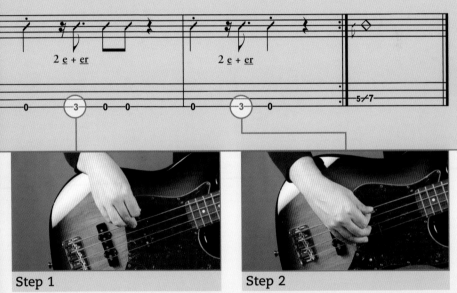

Step 1

Use alternate fingerstyle technique wherever possible. Play the second note in the first bar with "m."

Step 2

If you're playing this with a pick, use alternate picking ensuring that your up-picks fall on the "e" and "er." The photo illustrates the second note of the second bar played with an up-pick.

Continued over the page >>>

Example 2
The fourth sixteenth note is difficult to get right because it falls so late in the beat. Notice how quickly the third note follows the second in the first bar. Although the sixteenth note count is only written on the second beat, maintain this count throughout so that you won't have to subdivide the beat and clap a sixteenth note.

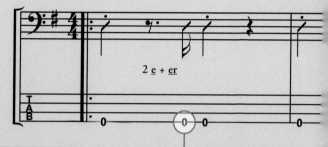

$\bullet = 80$

2 e + er

Step 1
This photo shows the second note in the first bar being played with "m." Notice the first finger (i) moving across the string to reach the note that swiftly follows.

Step 2
Pick playing also involves a strict alternate technique. Remember that any note on "er" should be played with an up-pick. Here you can see the second note of the second bar correctly played with an up-pick.

On the CD Track 44

Listen up!

Sixteenth notes

Sixteenth notes are similar to eighth notes in that they can be grouped together by a beam. Of course, sixteenth notes are "beamed" together by two lines rather than one. The chances are that one day you will encounter thirty-second and sixty-fourth notes as well, which are beamed together by three and four lines respectively, so it's a good idea to familiarize yourself with this style of notation.

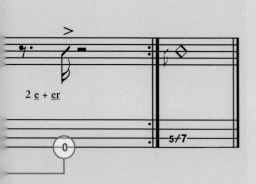

Listen up!

Counting sixteenth notes

To count sixteenth-rhythms correctly, add "e" and "er" on the offbeat sixteenth notes (i.e. the second and fourth notes).

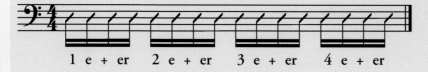

Continued over the page >>>

Example 3
Finally, both sixteenth-note syncopations are combined in the second bar of this example. To avoid mistakes and frustration, it's important that you are completely confident with examples 1 and 2 before you attempt this example.

$\flat$ = 80

2 <u>e</u> + <u>er</u>

Step 1

All of the notes in this example are played staccato (short). To achieve this effect, lightly touch the fourth string with the fingers flat as shown.

Step 2

Because these two sixteenth notes are so close together in the second bar, play them using "i" and "m." The photo shows the first sixteenth-note correctly played with "i."

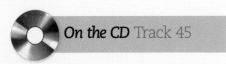

On the CD Track 45

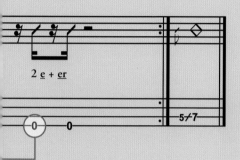

2 <u>e</u> + <u>er</u>

5ﾉ7

Listen up!

Grace notes

Grace notes (so-called because they "grace" or decorate the note they precede) are notes that are so short in duration that they are not assigned a rhythmic value. On the page, they look like eighth notes that have shrunk in the wash! Play them just before the "proper," full-size note that follows, with as small a gap as possible, but remember: it should sound graceful and smooth. If both the grace note and the following note are on the same string, pick only the grace note and slide to the "proper" note.

Lock like a rock

As a bassist, it's your job to lock with the drummer and stay as solid as a rock. That can be difficult when the keyboardist is playing a syncopated rhythm, or if the guitarist suddenly decides to play triplets! At times like these, it's important to remember the basic groove of what you're playing, even if that means counting "one-and-two-and-three..." to yourself as you play.

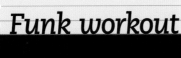

26 *Funk workout*

The term "funk" describes a wide range of music. It all began with the "Godfather" of funk—the late, great James Brown—in the early 1960s.

Jazz influences had crept in by the end of the sixties so that by the seventies, Stevie Wonder was busy creating a new brand of pop-funk, while the funk band Tower of Power nailed the tightest, trickiest, and slickest grooves that had ever been heard—with horns too! By the end of the decade funk had even found its way on to the New York disco floors with bands like Chic and Sister Sledge. Check out the discography to your right for some classic funk albums guaranteed to get your feet tapping!

*"Godfather of Soul" and
"King of Funk:" James
Brown performing live
at the Hammersmith
Apollo in London.*

Add it to your downloads!

The role of the bass in funk

The bass is the most important instrument in funk music. It locks with the drums and uses heavy syncopation (the emphasis of weak beats) to create infectious dance grooves. Funk tunes often begin as a jam between the bass and drums—the bass player comes up with a riff, the drummer lays down the groove and everything else is just icing sugar.

James Brown
20 All-time Greatest Hits!
Featured in *Rolling Stone* magazine's "greatest 500 albums of all time," this is a must-have for any serious funk aficionado.

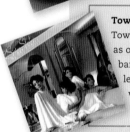

Stevie Wonder
Songs in the Key of Life
Packed with some stunning hits that feature great bass playing, this is widely regarded as Mr Wonder's greatest album. Get it in your collection!

Tower of Power *Back to Oakland*
Tower of Power are recognized as one of the greatest funk bands of all time, thanks to the legendary Rocco Prestia, who took bass guitar music to a whole new level.

Sister Sledge
The Best of Sister Sledge
The writing, producing, and playing partnership of guitarist Nile Rodgers and bassist Bernard Edwards dominated the dance charts in the late 1970s and early 1980s. Check out Chic's "Good Times" (later sampled and reworked as "Rapper's Delight") for one of the best funk basslines ever written.

Continued over the page >>>

Step 1

Fret the second note in bar one with your third finger.

Step 2

Play the two notes at the end of bar two with your first finger.

On the CD Tracks 46–47

Top tip

Heavy sixteenth-note syncopation
is what fuels any supercharged funk
bassline, and it's gotta be tight and
groovin'. This means you must have a
full understanding of the rhythm.

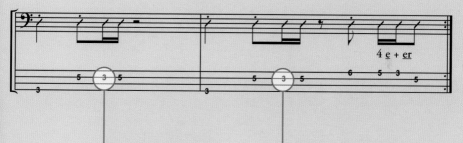

Step 3

Play the third note of bar three with your second finger (m).

Step 4

If you play this exercise with a pick, make sure you use alternate picking to play the third and fourth notes in the fourth bar.

Continued over the page >>>

Step 5

Fret the third note of bar five using your first finger.

Step 6

As you play the fifth note in bar six, stretch out your left hand a little to be ready for the approaching note on the fourth fret.

On the CD Tracks 46–47

Step 7

This picture shows the first finger (i) at rest on the neighboring string as the second finger plays the fourth note of bar seven.

Step 8

There is a stretch for the left hand at the end of bar eight as the fourth finger plays the final note on the fourth string.

The reggae groove

The bass and drums are the most important instruments in reggae; together they create the reggae rhythm—or "riddim" as it's known.

Feeling groovy

Reggae has a groove like no other: the first beat of the bar is often avoided; there's a heavy accent on the third beat; and eighth notes are often played with a swing feel (just like blues or jazz). In this lesson we'll be checking out the two basic reggae grooves: the one-drop and the stepper's beat. The one-drop is characterized by an empty first beat (hence its name), and has a kick and snare accent on the third—a rhythm that's entirely unique to reggae. The stepper's beat adds the kick on every beat (sometimes called "four on the floor") to create a driving groove. Reggae music sounds deceptively simple, but like most genres there's much more to it than the casual listener realizes.

Example 1

This is the "one-drop" reggae groove with the kick and snare falling on the third beat. Notice how the bass starts on the offbeat and locks with the kick on beat three—a typical phrasing for reggae basslines. Don't forget that the reggae groove is like no other, so don't be impatient if you can't "feel it" straight away.

𝅘𝅥 = 130

Step 1

Rest the palm of your right hand gently on the strings just in front of the bridge and use your thumb to play the first note as shown.

On the CD Tracks 48–49

See also: The reggae workout on page 158

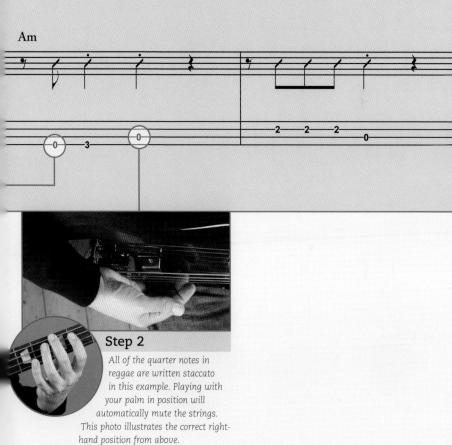

Step 2

All of the quarter notes in reggae are written staccato in this example. Playing with your palm in position will automatically mute the strings. This photo illustrates the correct right-hand position from above.

Continued over the page >>>

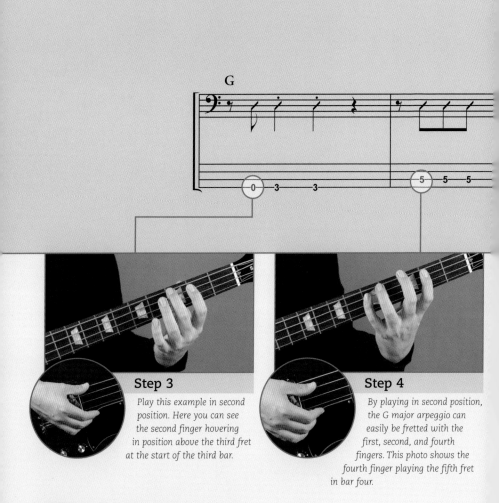

Step 3

Play this example in second position. Here you can see the second finger hovering in position above the third fret at the start of the third bar.

Step 4

By playing in second position, the G major arpeggio can easily be fretted with the first, second, and fourth fingers. This photo shows the fourth finger playing the fifth fret in bar four.

On the CD Tracks 48–49

Listen up!

Reggae fingerstyle
Reggae bass players usually play with their thumb only, muting the strings by lightly resting the palm of their picking hand just in front of the bridge. This creates that wonderful muffled reggae sound. While you can play these examples with pick or fingers, you will create a more authentic sound by using your thumb (playing downstrokes only) and by applying palm muting.

Continued over the page >>>

Example 2

The stepper's groove places the kick drum on each beat with a heavy accent on the third. Notice how the drum fills always end on the fourth beat with a cymbal crash. As drum fills generally always finish on the first beat in other styles of music, this can feel a bit unsettling at first.

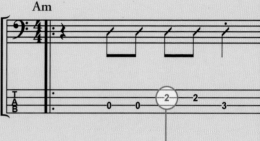

Step 1

Palm muting should also be applied when playing a stepper's groove. Here you can see the hand in position while the thumb picks the second string in the first bar. Make sure your palm is resting on all the strings as shown.

Step 2

The triplet figure at the start of the second bar is played with three quick down-picks. Notice how the thumb briefly touches the second string at the end of its stroke on the first note.

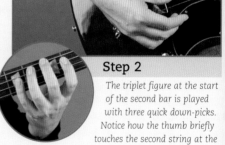

On the CD Tracks 50–51

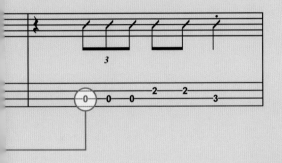

Listen up!

Eighth-note triplets

A triplet is three notes squashed into the space of two. So when you see a group of three notes with the "3" above them (any note can be played as a triplet) you need to play them quicker than normal. Start slowly as you would with any new concept, using the conventional "one-trip-let, two-trip-let" counting method, as shown below.

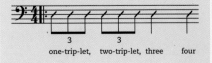

one-trip-let, two-trip-let, three   four

Continued over the page >>>

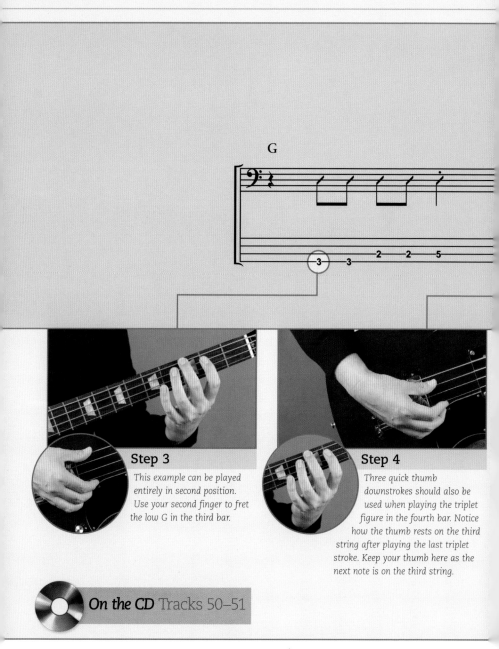

G

Step 3

This example can be played entirely in second position. Use your second finger to fret the low G in the third bar.

Step 4

Three quick thumb downstrokes should also be used when playing the triplet figure in the fourth bar. Notice how the thumb rests on the third string after playing the last triplet stroke. Keep your thumb here as the next note is on the third string.

On the CD Tracks 50–51

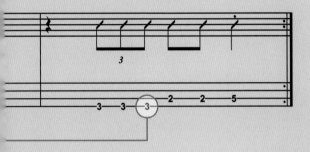

Listen up!

Drummers
Although practicing with
recordings or a metronome
is a very good thing, nothing
beats playing with a real life
flesh-and-blood drummer.
A famous bassist once said
that one hour playing in a
live band is worth a day of
practicing on your own, so
if you know someone who
plays the drums, get dialing!

28 *Reggae workout*

Reggae is a Jamaican music born out of ska and rocksteady in the late 1960s. Work out to this and you'll be "linking" and "skanking" in no time!

In the early 1960s, the Jamaican "rudeboys" (characterized by their sharp suits, thin ties, and pork pie hats) started playing ska records at half speed as they felt that the cooler, slower dance tempo was more in keeping with their tough image. This style was picked up on by Jamaican musicians who in turn began to slow down the tempo of their tunes: and so rocksteady was born. This short-lived genre was superseded by reggae between 1967 and 1968.

The reggae groove has an ambiguous half-time feel that can be counted with an accent on the third beat, or with kick and snare accents falling on the second and fourth beats. Controversy still reigns over exactly how

"Feeling the groove:" the legendary Bob Marley performing live. Marley was a great pioneer of Jamaican reggae music in the 1960s, and those heavy dreads have since gained iconic status.

Add it to your downloads!

reggae should be counted. Reggae musicians, however, never read what they are playing; this music is all about "feeling the groove."

The role of the bass in reggae

In the previous lesson (starting on page 150), we looked at the two dominant grooves in reggae: the one-drop rhythm and the stepper's beat. The bass' role in both is the same, providing a percussive, palm-muted line that avoids the first beat and locks with the kick on the accented third beat. Basslines are frequently arpeggio based (not dissimilar to jazz) and it is quite common for one guitarist to double the bassline an octave higher (the "link") while the other guitarist plays an offbeat percussive rhythm (the "skank").

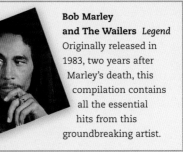

Bob Marley and The Wailers *Legend*
Originally released in 1983, two years after Marley's death, this compilation contains all the essential hits from this groundbreaking artist.

Peter Tosh *Legalize It*
The original guitarist with Bob Marley in the Wailing Wailers, Peter Tosh quit the group in 1974 to pursue a solo career. This album was Tosh's second solo release and contains some outstanding reggae grooves. When the album was first released in 1976 it featured a marijuana scented sticker!

Sly and Robbie
Riddim: Best of Sly & Robbie in Dub
Drummer Lowell "Sly" Dunbar and bassist Robert Shakespeare were the session players on countless reggae hits throughout the 1970s and 1980s. Sly Dunbar's first hit was "Liquidator," recorded when he was just 14! The recording and producing duo are masters of the dub style, and use remixing and effects extensively.

Top tip

For that authentic reggae bass sound turn up the bass control on your amp and turn down the tone control on your bass.

Continued over the page >>>

Example 1

This sparse but rhythmically challenging bassline incorporates both the one-drop and stepper's grooves. Pick the notes with your thumb, keeping your palm resting on the strings throughout as illustrated.

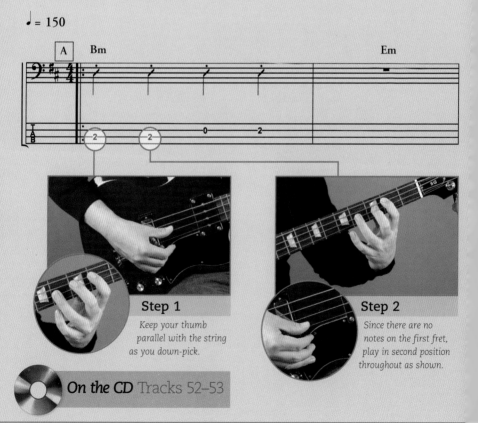

♩ = 150

A Bm   Em

Step 1

Keep your thumb parallel with the string as you down-pick.

Step 2

Since there are no notes on the first fret, play in second position throughout as shown.

On the CD Tracks 52–53

▸▸ **See also:** The reggae groove on page 150

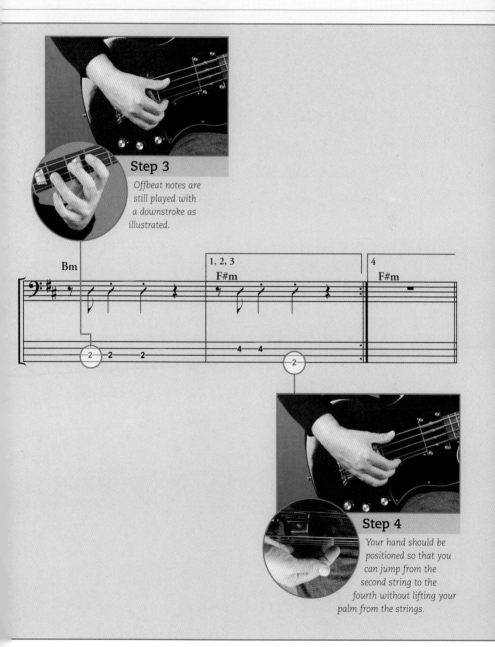

Step 3

Offbeat notes are still played with a downstroke as illustrated.

Bm

1, 2, 3
F#m

4
F#m

Step 4

Your hand should be positioned so that you can jump from the second string to the fourth without lifting your palm from the strings.

Continued over the page >>>

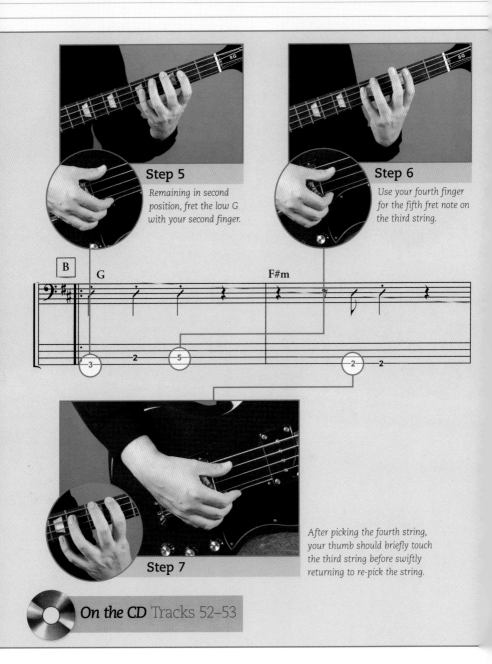

Step 5

Remaining in second position, fret the low G with your second finger.

Step 6

Use your fourth finger for the fifth fret note on the third string.

Step 7

After picking the fourth string, your thumb should briefly touch the third string before swiftly returning to re-pick the string.

On the CD Tracks 52–53

Top tip

This arrangement should be played with your thumb. Fingerstyle and pickstyle techniques won't enable you to mute the strings.

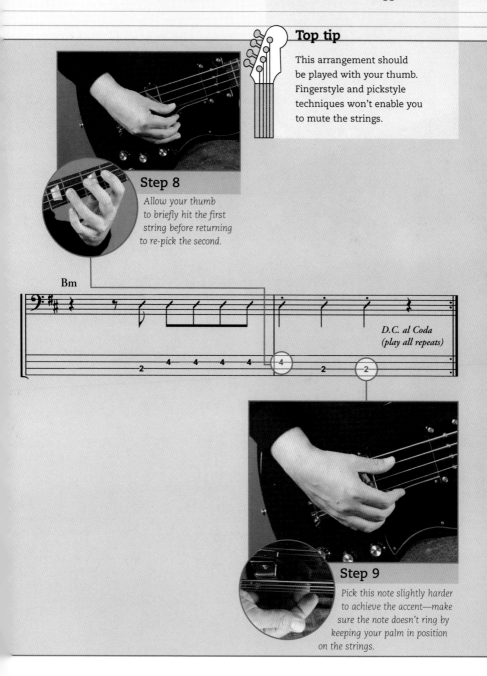

Step 8

Allow your thumb to briefly hit the first string before returning to re-pick the second.

Bm

D.C. al Coda (play all repeats)

Step 9

Pick this note slightly harder to achieve the accent—make sure the note doesn't ring by keeping your palm in position on the strings.

How to pass your first audition

So, now you've got your chops together and you're ready to start gigging. There's just one problem—you need a band.

One option is to form your own group with your friends, but this can be a longwinded and tiresome process. Could you handle firing the drummer (who may be your best buddy) because he's got no sense of rhythm? It could be months before you can even think about gigging. It's much simpler to join an established band.

Bands fall into two categories: original and covers. If you want to gain experience fast and earn some cash while you do it, opt for the latter. The covers band usually play a mixed repertoire (e.g. soul, rock 'n' roll, funk) and are likely to be a semi-pro outfit, unless they are a tribute band dedicated to playing only one group's material. Choose your covers band wisely and according to your music taste: the more popular the original band, the more likely you are to find a band playing their covers.

ass Player Wanted Five
piece band urgently require
committed bass player. We
play a range of covers from
Bryan Adams, Fleetwood
Mac, The Commitments,
Bad Co, etc. A sense of
humour and your own gear
are essential. Own hair and
teeth optional. Call Jimmy
on 121 212121.

Punk Band need manager

Wanted!

Check your local newspaper for "musician wanted" ads. Many "free ad" papers also have a music section. Don't forget to browse online too—sites range from the local, to the global www.starnow.com. Music shops and music colleges usually have a musicians' bulletin or message board—check them out regularly. Why not place your own ad while you're there?

The audition checklist

Auditions are notoriously tough experiences, and every musician has a horror story to tell. However, you mustn't be dissuaded from trying. Naturally, you will be nervous and you probably won't play your very best, but this handy checklist will make sure you give it your best shot, and don't leave anything to chance on the day.

1 Find out as much as you can about the band beforehand. Write a list of questions that you want answers to before you get in contact. How long have they been together? How many gigs do they do? What areas do they play in? How much money do they earn on average per gig? Where do they rehearse (and will this cost you money)?

2 Find out what you will be expected to play. If this is the band you really want to join, learn a couple of songs before the audition. And don't forget to check what key they play them in (cover bands will often change songs from the original key to suit the singer's voice).

3 Find out if you need to take your own gear, or if there will be a bass amp there you can use. Take your own instrument even if you don't have to—there's nothing worse than trying to play on a strange bass when you're nervous!

4 Tune up. If you haven't got a tuner, buy one—you're going to need it. Don't launch into the song without tuning up first: it will sound terrible however well you play it. There's nothing worse than an out of tune bass—it makes the whole band sound out of tune and you'll be sacked before you even get the job.

5 Be early! If you can't turn up on time for the audition you probably won't turn up on time for gigs either. It doesn't matter how good you are—if you stumble in late you're unlikely to get the gig.

6 Be aware of your volume. If you play too loudly or too quietly you are not going to sound convincing or effective. If you're using a hired amp, familiarize yourself with the controls before you start and don't be afraid to change the settings mid-song—this is a perfectly acceptable thing to do.

7 Look the part. Every band has some kind of image. If you're auditioning for a metal band, you don't want to turn up looking like a country and western fan!

Scale Library

You'll find this chapter to be a useful and essential resource when learning to play the bass guitar. These basic scales, arranged chromatically for easy reference, are shown in their shape-1 and shape-4 variations. To encourage quick and easy learning, a diagramatic fingerboard indicates where, and in which order, to place your fingers when tackling each scale. Learn these, and you'll begin to feel more confident in improvisation sessions with your bandmates.

C major *shape 1*

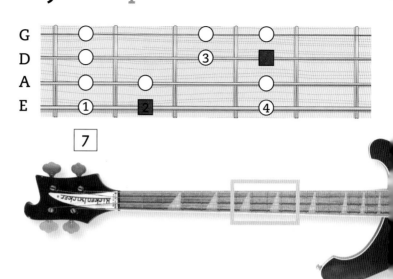

shape 4

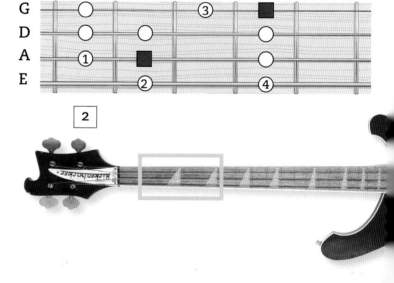

C natural minor *shape 1*

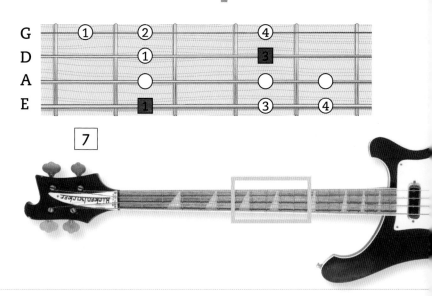

shape 4

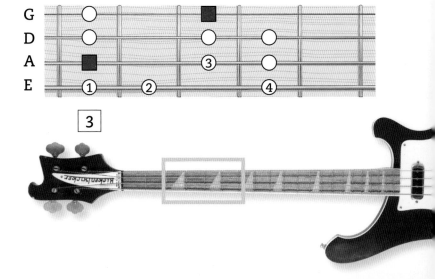

C minor pentatonic *shape 1*

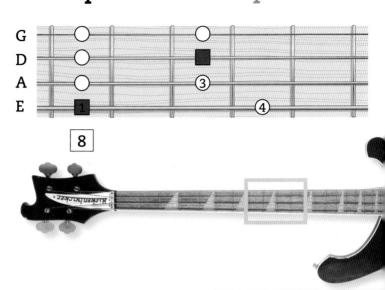

shape 4

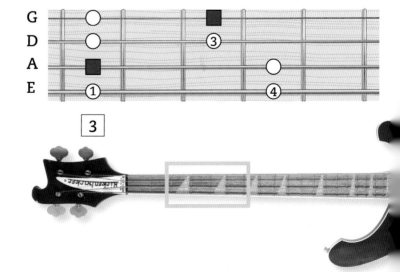

C blues *shape 1*

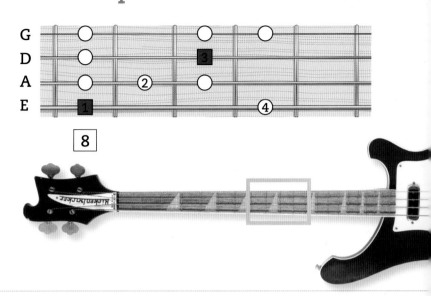

shape 4

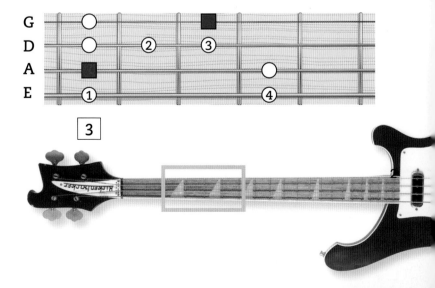

C#/D♭ major *shape 1*

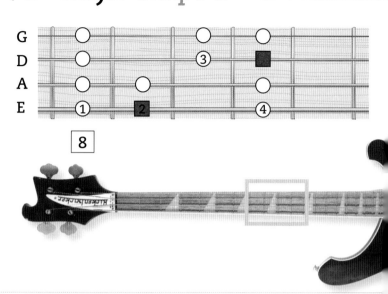

shape 4

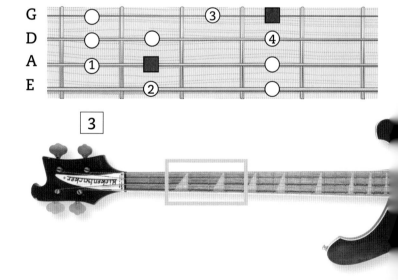

C♯/D♭ *natural minor shape 1*

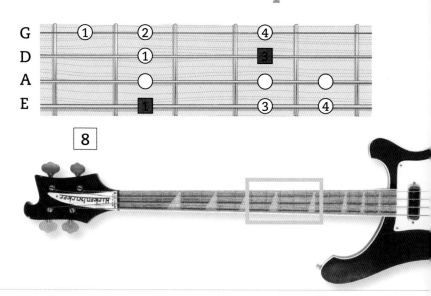

shape 4

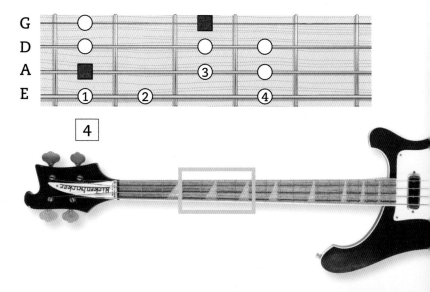

C♯/D♭ minor pentatonic *shape 1*

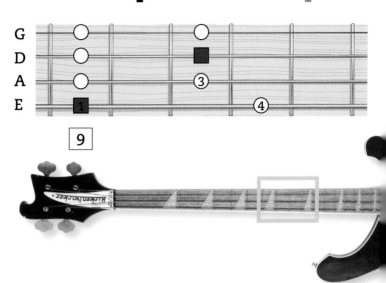

shape 4

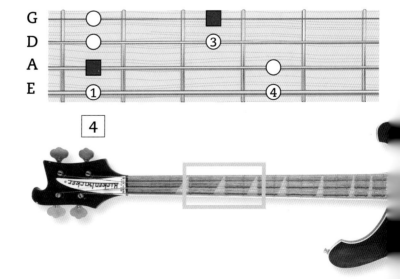

C#/D♭ **blues** *shape 1*

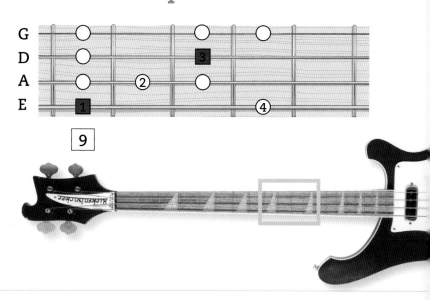

shape 4

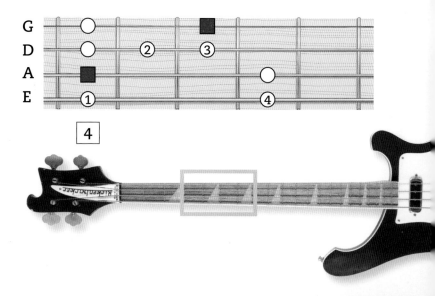

D major *shape 1*

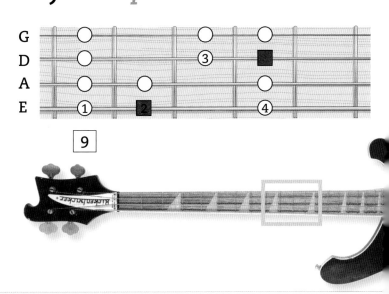

shape 4

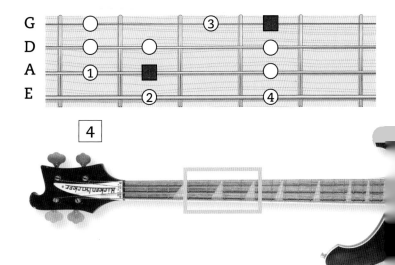

D natural minor *shape 1*

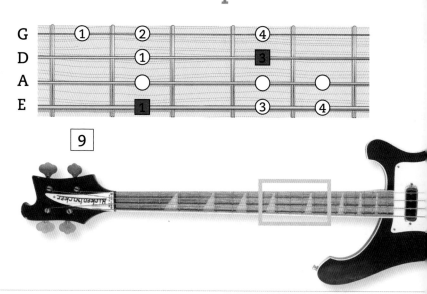

shape 4

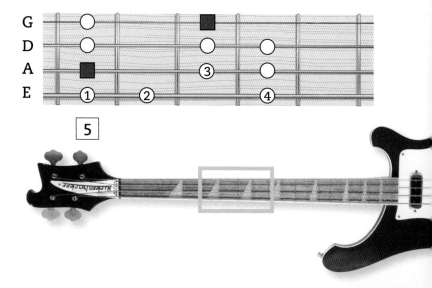

D minor pentatonic *shape 1*

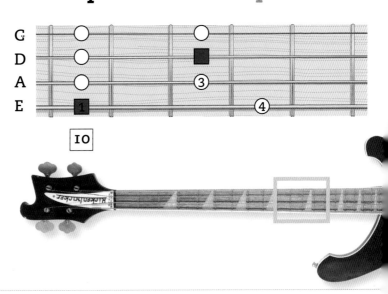

shape 4

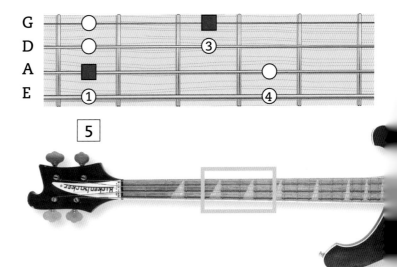

D blues *shape 1*

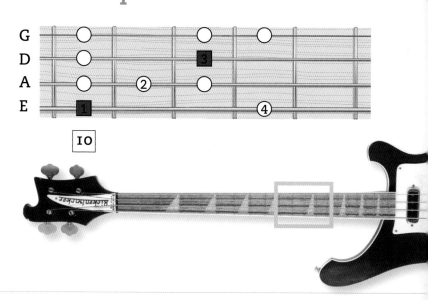

shape 4

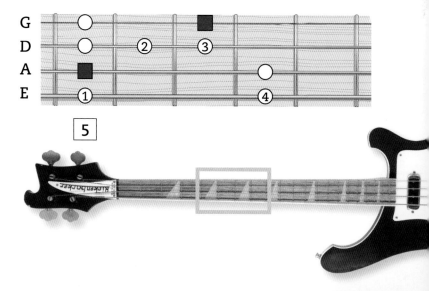

D#/E♭ major shape 1

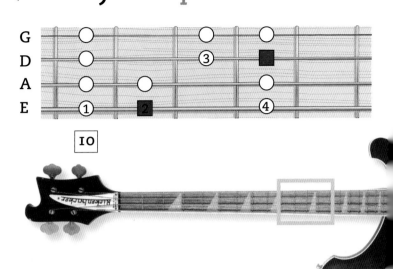

shape 4

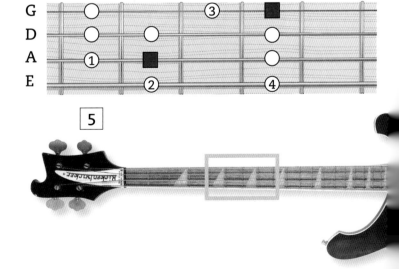

D♯/E♭ *natural minor shape 1*

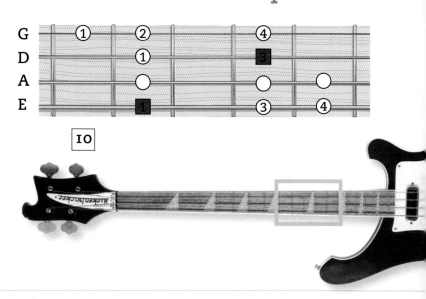

shape 4

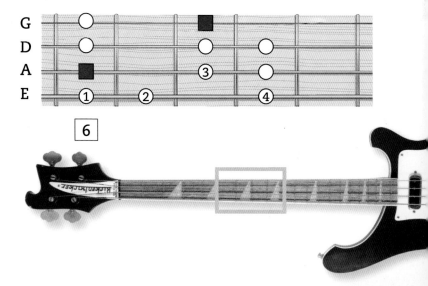

D♯/E♭ minor pentatonic *shape 1*

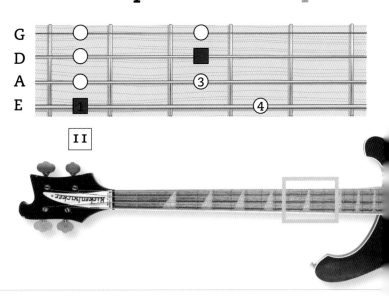

shape 4

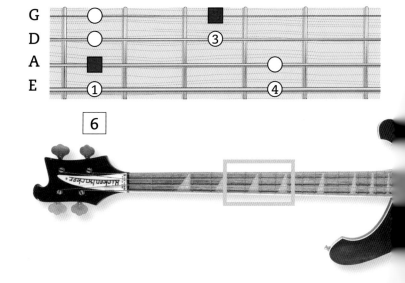

D♯/E♭ blues *shape 1*

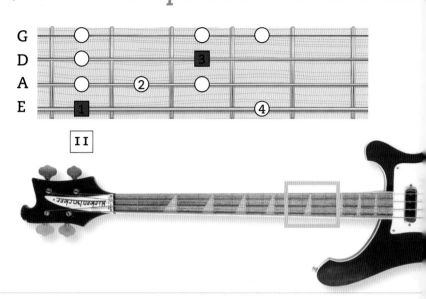

shape 4

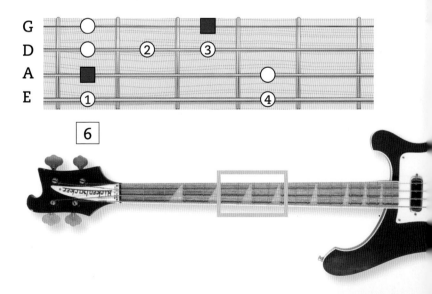

E major *shape 1*

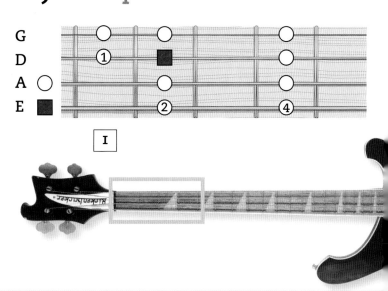

shape 4

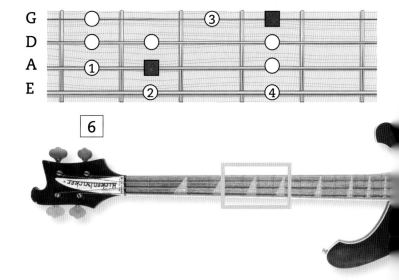

E natural minor *shape 1*

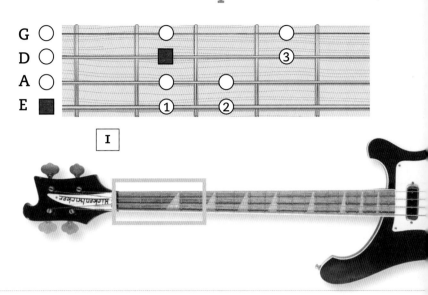

shape 4

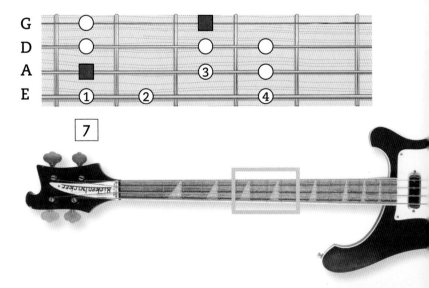

E minor pentatonic *shape 1*

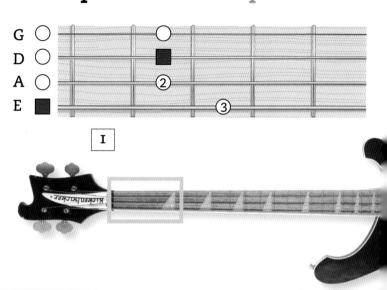

shape 4

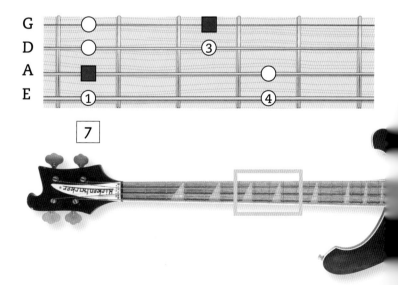

E blues *shape 1*

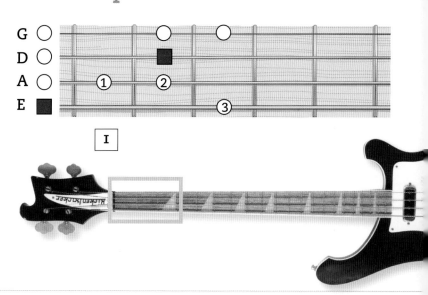

shape 4

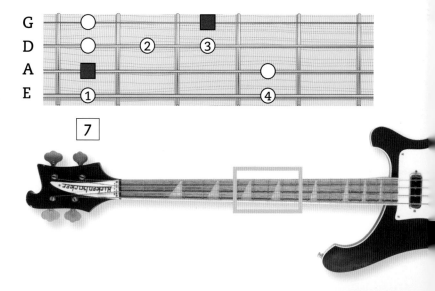

F major shape 1

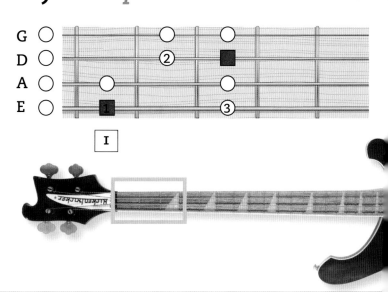

shape 4

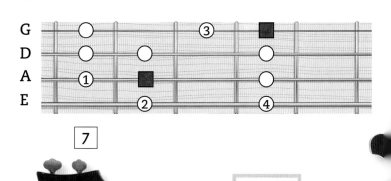

F natural minor *shape 1*

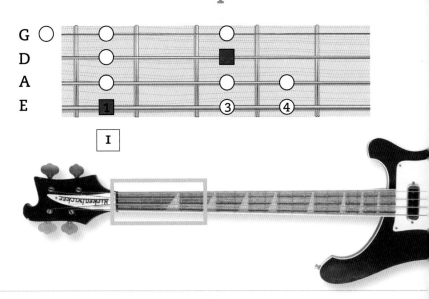

shape 4

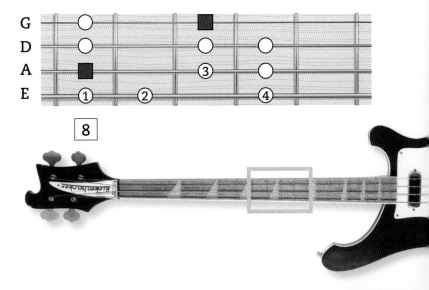

F minor pentatonic *shape 1*

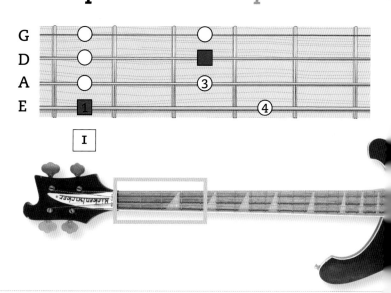

shape 4

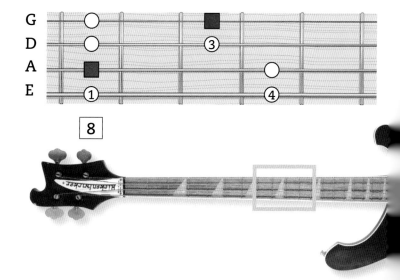

F blues *shape 1*

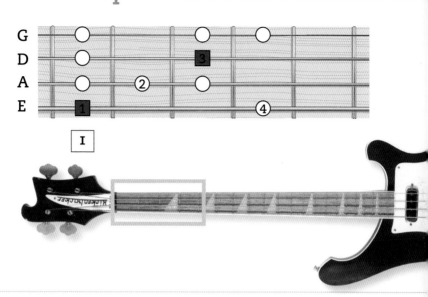

shape 4

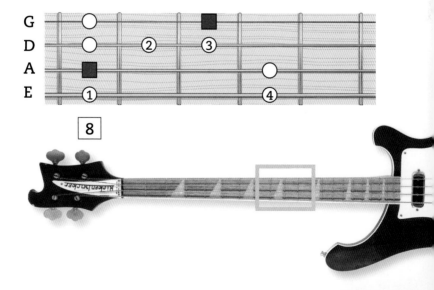

F#/G♭ *major* *shape 1*

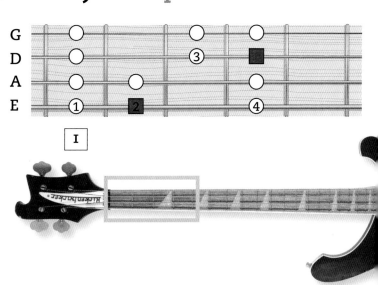

I

shape 4

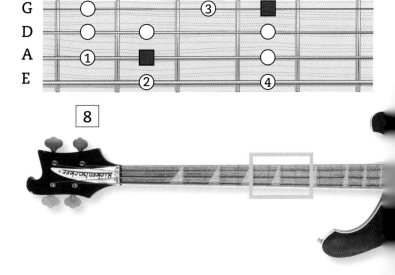

8

F#/G♭ *natural minor shape 1*

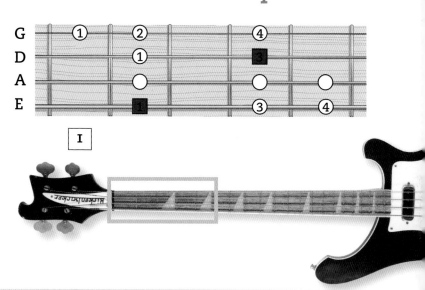

shape 4

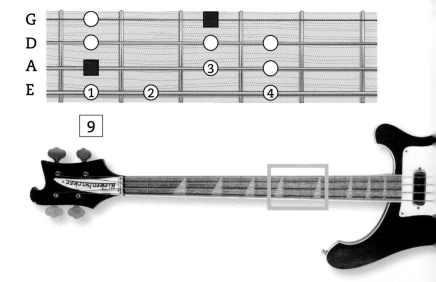

F#/G♭ minor pentatonic *shape 1*

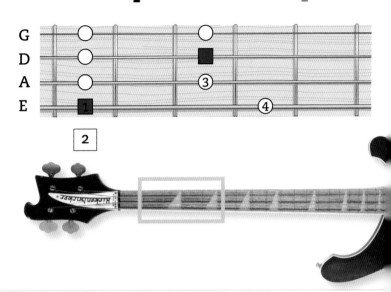

shape 4

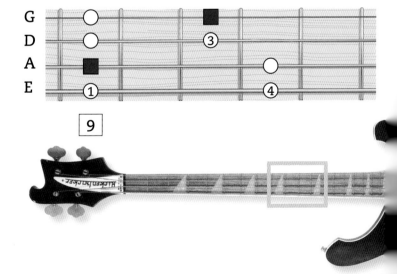

F#/G♭ blues *shape 1*

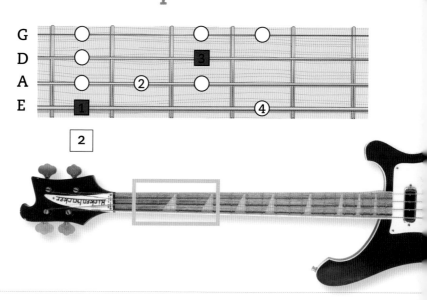

shape 4

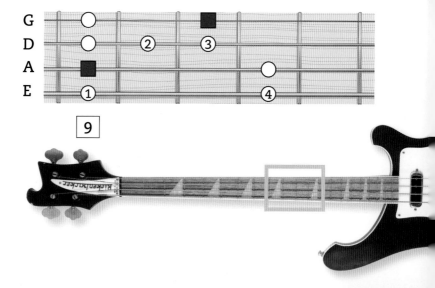

G major *shape 1*

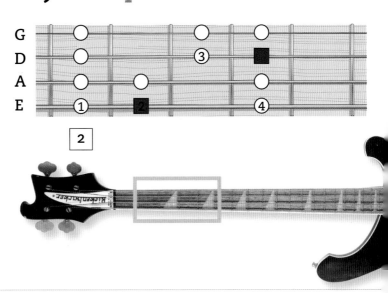

shape 4

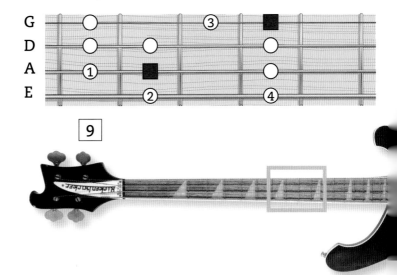

G natural minor *shape 1*

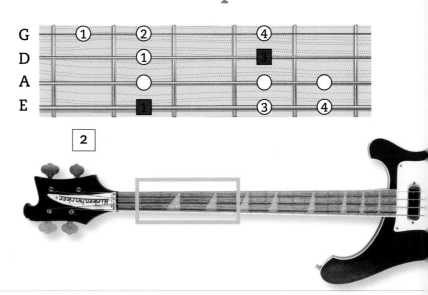

shape 4

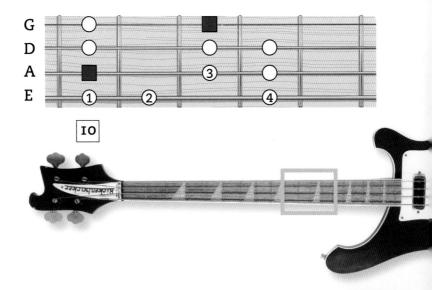

G minor pentatonic *shape 1*

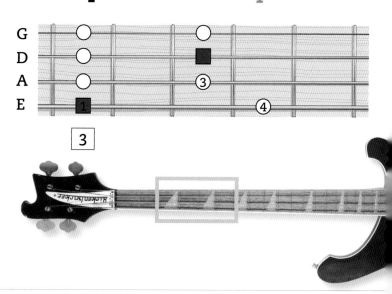

shape 4

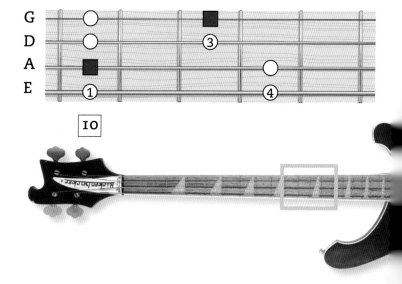

G blues *shape 1*

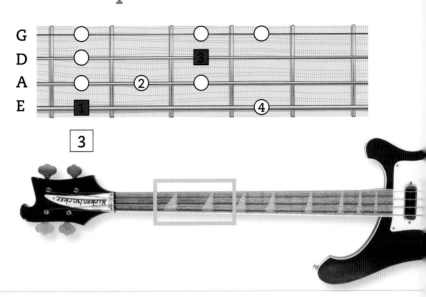

shape 4

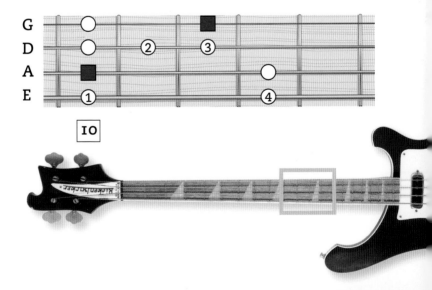

G#/Ab *major* *shape 1*

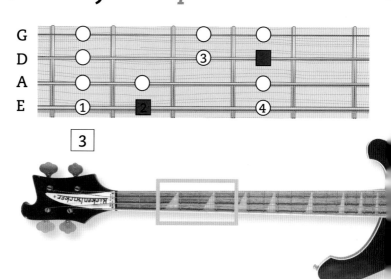

shape 4

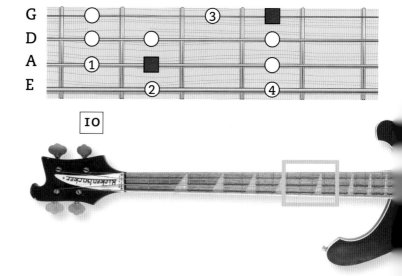

G#/A♭ natural minor *shape 1*

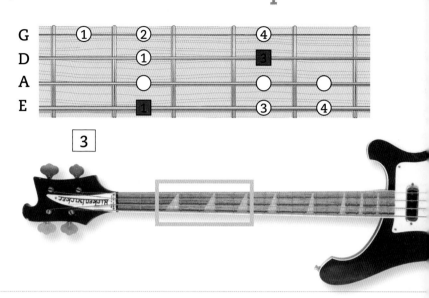

shape 4

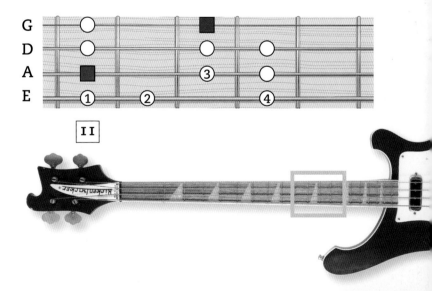

G♯/A♭ minor pentatonic *shape 1*

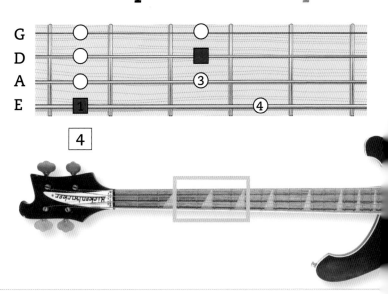

shape 4

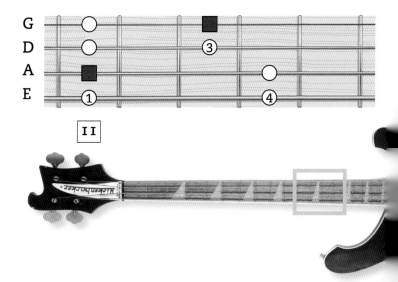

G♯/A♭ *blues shape 1*

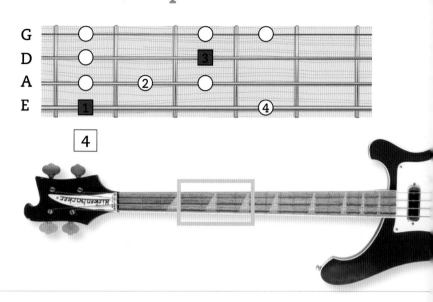

shape 4

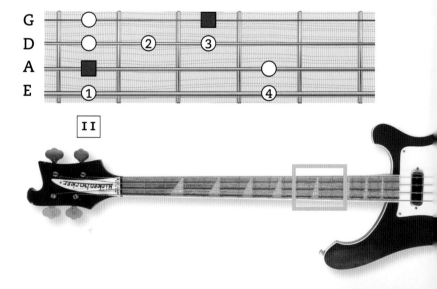

A major *shape 1*

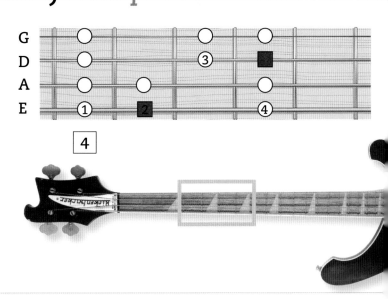

shape 4

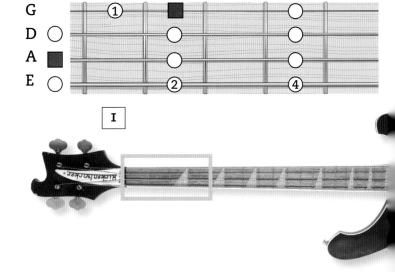

A *natural minor* *shape 1*

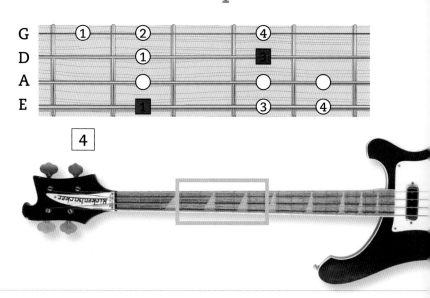

shape 4

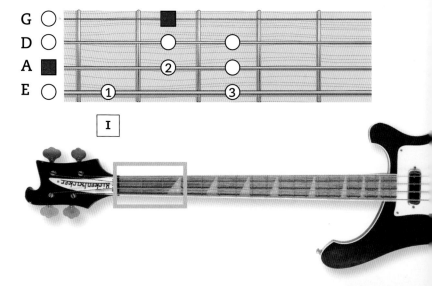

A minor pentatonic *shape 1*

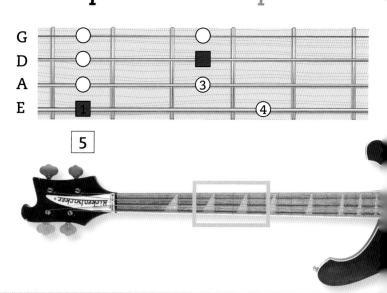

shape 4

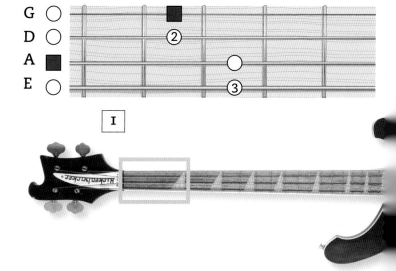

A blues *shape 1*

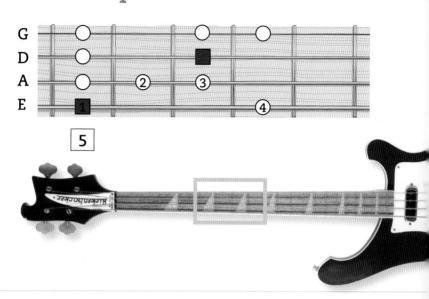

shape 4

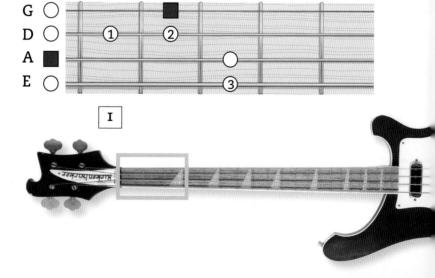

A#/B♭ *major shape 1*

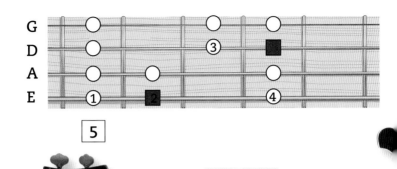

shape 4

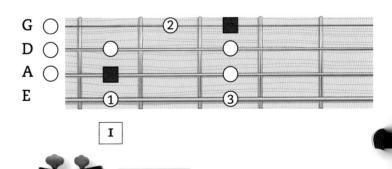

A#/B♭ natural minor *shape 1*

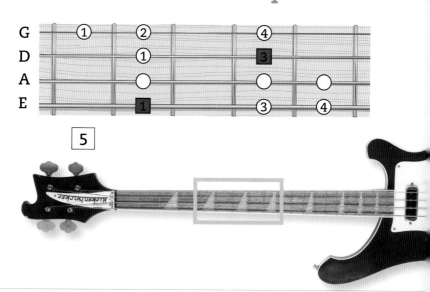

shape 4

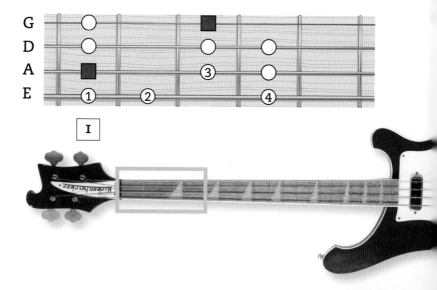

A#/B♭ *minor pentatonic* *shape 1*

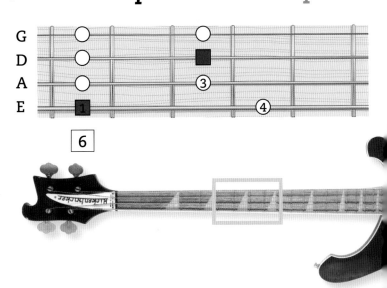

shape 4

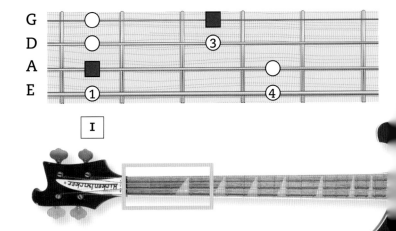

A#/B♭ *blues* shape 1

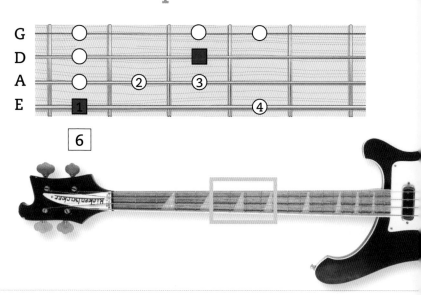

shape 4

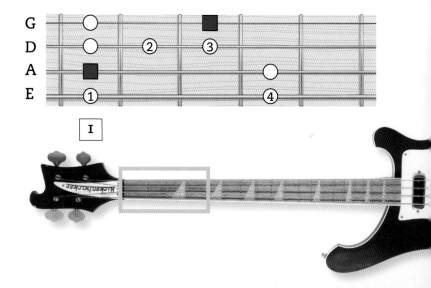

B major *shape 1*

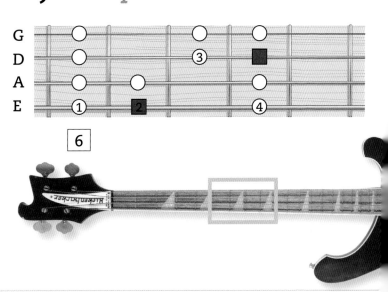

shape 4

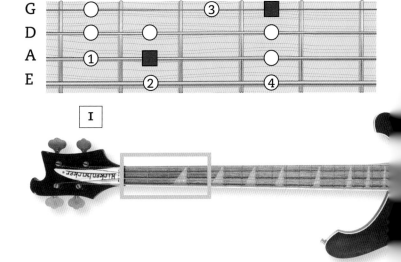

B natural minor *shape 1*

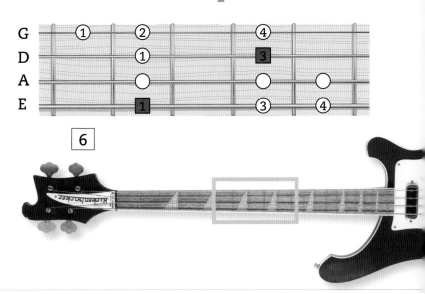

shape 4

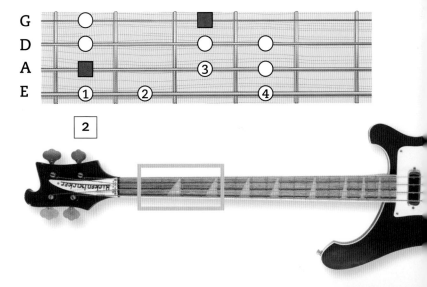

B minor pentatonic *shape 1*

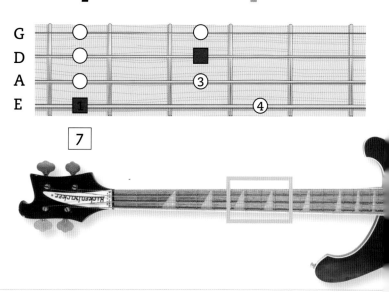

shape 4

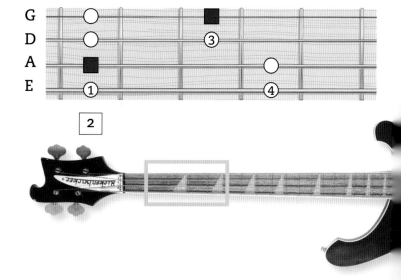

B blues *shape 1*

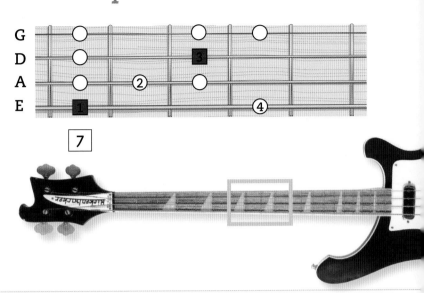

shape 4

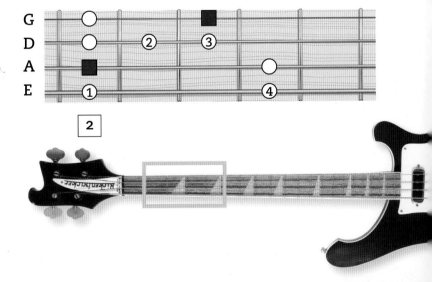

Arpeggio Library

Arpeggios are chords played melodically instead of harmonically. Learning to play arpeggios will greatly extend your knowledge and experience of notes, and how they sound when played together, giving you more opportunity for creative jamming in the rehearsal room. This section lists, chromatically, the arpeggios you are most likely to come across in your early days as a bass player. Only the shape-1 formation is given: learn these before you move on to more complex shapes and patterns, like the moveable arpeggios, detailed on pages 230–233.

C major

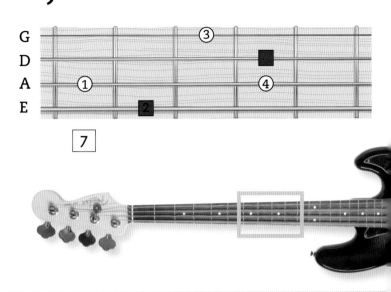

C minor

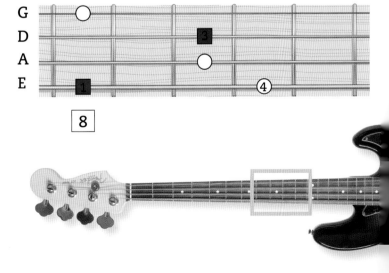

C#/Db *major*

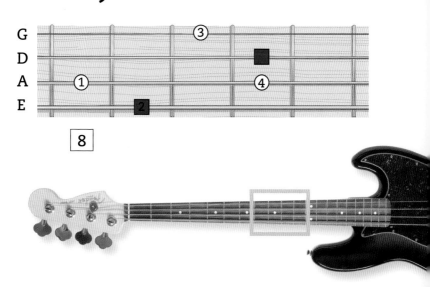

C#/Db *minor*

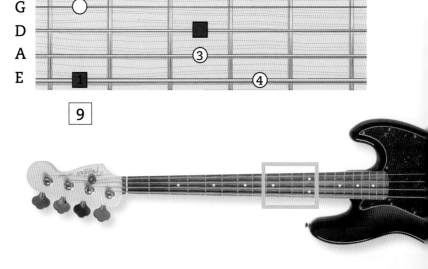

D major

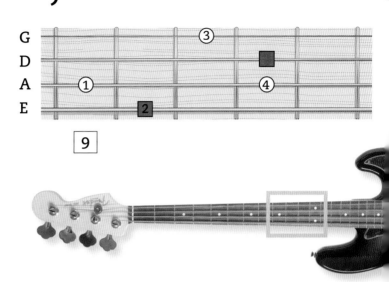

9

D minor

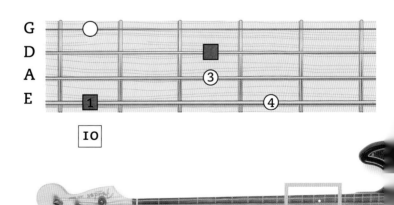

IO

D#/E♭ major

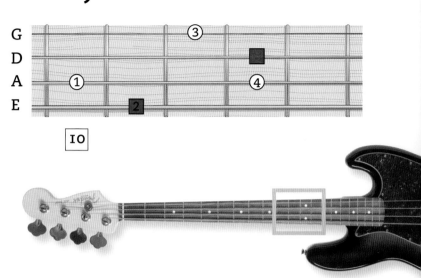

D#/E♭ minor

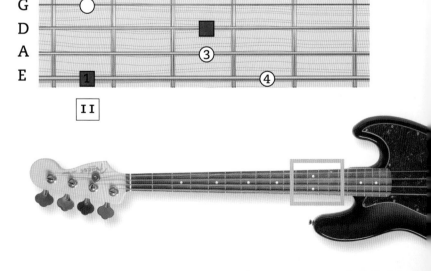

E major

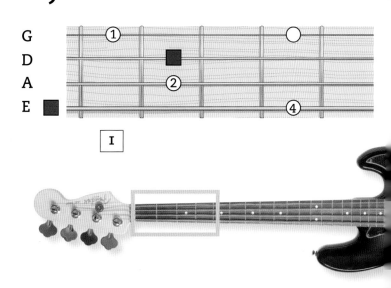

E minor

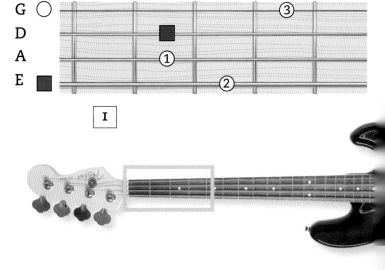

F major

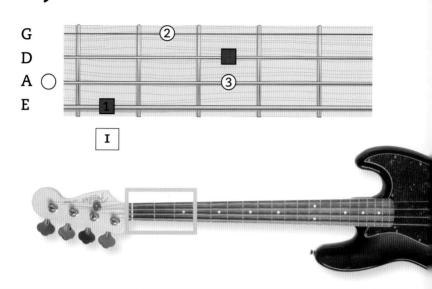

F minor

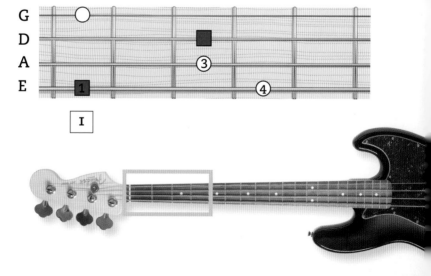

F♯/G♭ major

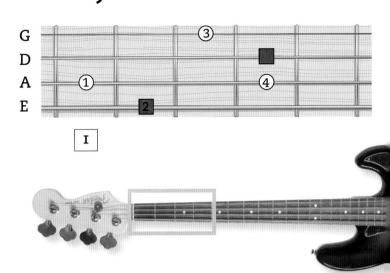

I

F♯/G♭ minor

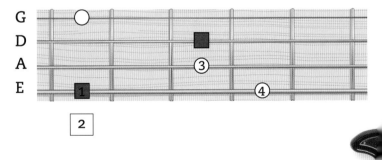

2

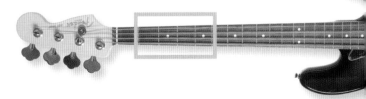

Arpeggio library

G major

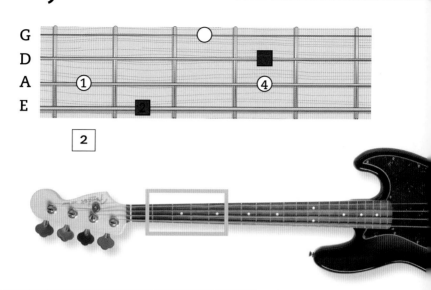

G minor

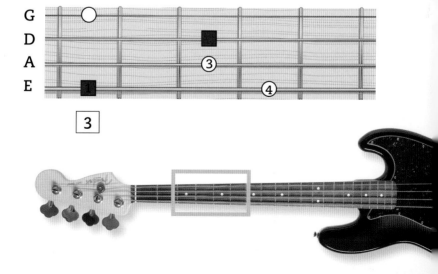

G#/A♭ major

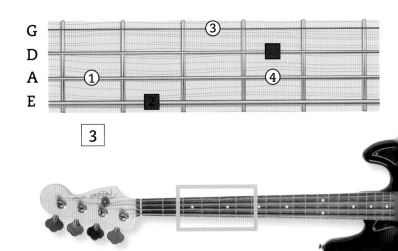

G#/A♭ minor

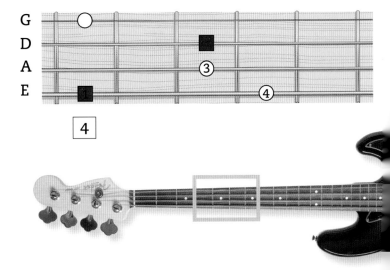

A major

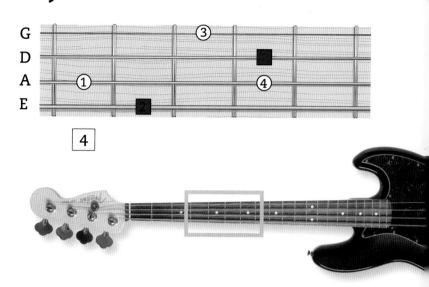

A minor

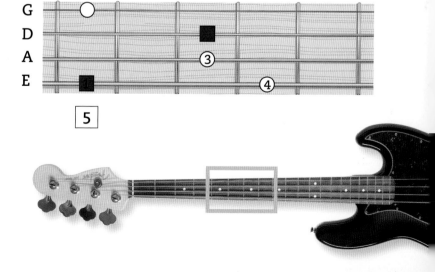

A#/B♭ major

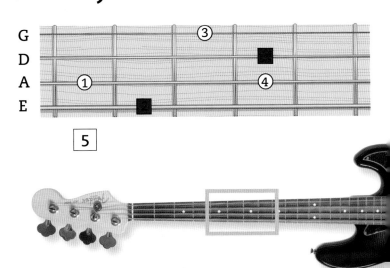

A#/B♭ minor

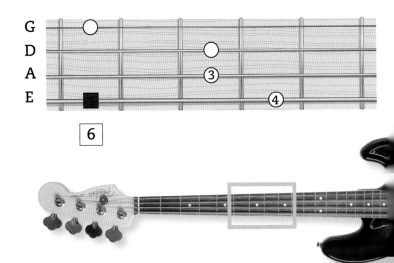

B major

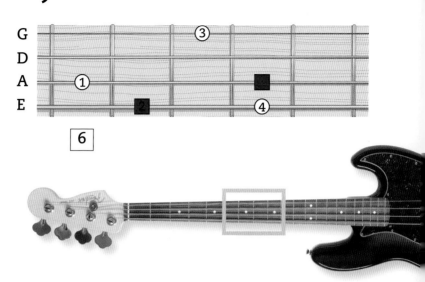

B minor

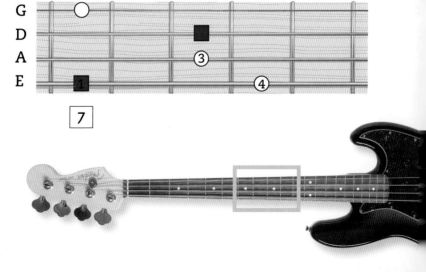

Minor 6 (min6, m6)

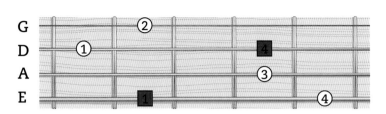

Minor 7(min7, m7)

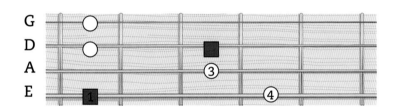

Minor 9 (min9, m9)

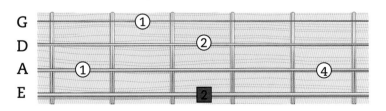

Moveable arpeggios

Minor 7♭5 (min7♭5, m7♭5, Δ)

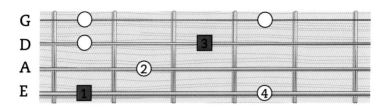

Major 6 (maj6, M6)

Major 7 (maj7, M7, Δ)

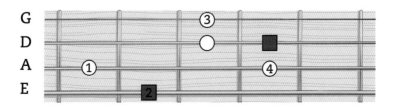

Major 9 (maj9, M9, Δ9)

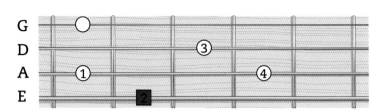

Major 7♭5 (maj7♭5, M7♭5, Δ♭5)

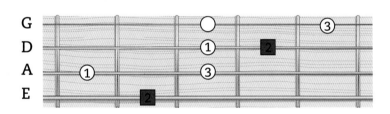

Dominant 7 (7, dom7)

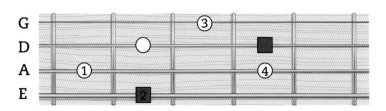

Moveable arpeggios

Dominant 9 (9, dom9)

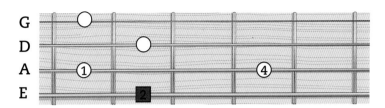

Augmented 7 (7+, 7#5, aug7)

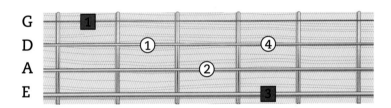

Diminished 7 (dim7, 7-)

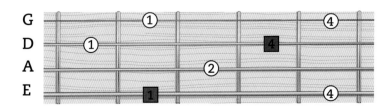

Buyer's Guide

This is your guide to locating and purchasing your bass guitar and accompanying bass equipment. Amps, tuners, guitar care, carry-cases, music stands, straps, strings, and metronomes: make sure you have all the essential gear to kickstart a life of gigging and touring, with your ideal bass.

Classic bass designs

Top five beginner basses

1 Fender Squire Affinity P-bass

2 Fender Squire Affinity J-bass

3 Epiphone EB-0

4 Yamaha RBX170

5 Ibanez GSR200

Fender Precision bass

The "P-bass" was the first mass-produced, solid-bodied electric bass. It went on sale in 1951 and has remained in production to this day.

Look and sound

With its one-piece body, bolt-on maple neck, and single humbucking pick-up, the P-bass is a pretty basic looking and sounding instrument, but it has remained one of the best-selling basses ever produced and its popularity shows no signs of waning.

Choosing a model

Fender currently offers a huge choice of models, from the budget Squire range to the expensive American Standard and Vintage series. The Squire Affinity P-bass is an ideal beginner's model and the cheapest option. More expensive, but offering excellent

Sheryl Crow rocks out at Wembley Arena, London with her Gibson Les Paul bass guitar.

value, is the "made in Mexico" Standard P-bass. These use cheaper parts than USA models, but they are significantly better than the Squires. The American Standard and American Vintage series are the "made in USA" real deal, but you pay an awful lot more for the privilege. One thing's for sure, if it's a P-bass you desire, you're guaranteed to find a model to suit your taste and budget.

Budgeting

Secondhand Fender guitars are only a cheaper option if produced in the last 15 years or less. Earlier models start to rise in value sharply, with 1970s Fenders now pioneering the high prices. Original 1950s models (even those in poor condition) are now way out of the reach of the average musician.

P-bass players

- John Paul Jones (Led Zeppelin)
- Cliff Burton (Metallica)
- Mike Dirnt (Green Day)
- Sting

Fender Jazz bass

Originally introduced to woo jazz players away from their double basses, the "J-bass" has remained virtually unchanged and in continuous production ever since its debut in 1960—bar a few minor cosmetic enhancements.

Look and sound

The J-bass is similar in look to the P-bass (see page 237), but it has a much wider range of tones since it's fitted with two single coil pick-ups. The slim, low-profile neck and contoured body make it more comfortable to play than the P-bass. You will notice that the J-bass also has a more pronounced mid-range tone. This was no accident; it was designed specifically to compete against the brighter-sounding Rickenbacker 4000 bass (introduced in 1957) that was challenging sales of the P-bass.

Choosing a model

Fender now produces a wide range of guitars. Its three-tier pricing starts with the Squire (Affinity J-bass), moves up to the Mexican models (Standard J-bass), and peaks with the USA-built American and American Vintage series.

Budgeting

The J-bass offers classic looks and a wide range of sounds, but because it is more expensive to produce than the P-bass, prices are higher than comparable P-bass models. If you don't need the extra tonal versatility of the J-bass, this may not necessarily be money well spent. However, there's no doubt that as your musical horizons widen, you can count on the J-bass to deliver any sound you'll need!

J-bass players

- Jaco Pastorius
- Marcus Miller
- Victor Bailey
- Noel Redding (Jimi Hendrix)
- Tim Commerford

Gibson EB/SG bass

Sadly, Gibson never enjoyed the widespread domination of the bass guitar market that Fender did with their "P-" and "J-" basses. To try and rectify the problem, the company introduced its third model, the EB0, in 1959.

Look and sound

The EB0 was essentially the twin-horned body from their new SG guitar range fitted with a short-scale bass neck and a single humbucking pick-up. The range was supplemented in 1961 by the EB3; its extra bridge pick-up gave this "deluxe" model a much brighter sound. With a solid mahogany body, one-piece mahogany neck, and an unbound 20-fret short scale neck, the bass was a practical, workman-like addition to Gibson's bass range, and it had a very distinctive sound. Recently, Gibson have reissued the EB3 as the "SG bass," which remains faithful to the original design except for two volume controls and a single tone which are utilized instead of the original varitone switch and quartet of controls.

Choosing a model

Because of its short neck, the SG bass is fast and easy to play; most models are a firm favorite with guitarists who play the occasional bit of bass.

Budgeting

The thin-bodied, simple design of the SG is easy to manufacture and, although it isn't cheap, it offers exceptional value for money for a genuine, "made in USA," vintage spec instrument. If you're not ready to invest in a Gibson just yet, check out the Epiphone EB-0 and EB-3 models— these also feature a mahogany neck and body.

Gibson SG players

- Jack Bruce (Cream)
- Andy Fraser (Free)
- Bill Wyman (Rolling Stones)
- Jared Followill (Kings of Leon)

Rickenbacker 4001 stereo bass

The Rickenbacker 4001 bass
was first introduced in 1961
and was the company's
second electric model.

Look and sound

In 1971, the 4001 had two pick-ups
and a stereo "Ric-o-sound" option,
which added an extra output socket
(one for each pick-up). This gave
players the option of routing the
signal through two amps to achieve a
bigger sound. It featured the standard
Rickenbacker "thru neck" construction
(which produces greater sustain) and
twin truss rods (to enable neck twist
correction, in addition to the standard
curvature compensation). There is no
other bass that looks or sounds like
a Rickenbacker 4001; it's an iconic
instrument that many of
the world's bass pioneers
have made their own.
The last 4001 bass was
manufactured in 1984.
However, Rickenbacker
have recently re-introduced
the model (although not to
vintage spec) as the 4001C64
and 4001C64S (stereo
version).

Choosing a model

In the 1970s, copies of the
top guitar marques were
manufactured in Japan
and the Far East before
the big names clamped
down with a string of lawsuits. The best
Rickenbacker clones were made
by Ibanez, Maya, Univox and
Aria and were built to a high
standard—even the Ric-o-
sound option and twin truss
rods were available on some
models. If you're lucky you
may come across one of these
secondhand; if you do, snap it up!

Budgeting

Unfortunately, if you hanker after
one of these instruments, you will
have to pay a hefty price for one. The
company don't make budget models
and even secondhand 4001 models
in poor condition still demand a high
price. The newer 4003 models are
about the same price as the Fender
American series—but for a 4001C64S
(which is actually a replica of Paul
McCartney's current bass), just
double the price!

4001 players

- Paul McCartney
- Chris Squire (Yes)
- Geddy Lee (Rush)
- Bruce Foxton (The Jam)
- Chris Ross (Wolfmother)

Music Man StingRay bass

The relatively new Music Man Company evolved out of the collaboration between Leo Fender and Tom Walker (a dissatisfied post-CBS Fender sales rep). The company's first instruments were produced in 1976: the StingRay guitar and bass series.

Look and sound

While the guitar version languished, the StingRay bass (with its unusual lop-sided headstock design) became an instant success. Despite the fact that the Music Man brand was purchased by the Ernie Ball Company in 1984, the StingRay bass has remained in constant production since its introduction. The original StingRay was the first instrument to feature an active EQ preamp system (powered by an internal battery). This could boost specific frequencies instead of simply reducing them, as the traditional "tone pot" design had done; it gave the instrument a huge tonal range, despite being fitted with a single humbucker pick-up. Today, the StingRay is fitted with two humbucking pick-ups and is available in many variations including 5-string and

fretless models. All models continue to use the active preamp circuitry that countless bass manufacturers have since copied.

Choosing a model

As the model has been in production since 1976, secondhand instruments are not uncommon. Be aware that vintage guitars in good condition are often more expensive than new ones.

Budgeting

The StingRay bass is another expensive USA-made instrument that could seriously damage your credit card! Like Rickenbacker, the company doesn't produce budget alternatives. If, however, you're lucky enough to stumble across a reasonably priced secondhand StingRay, don't hesitate— they are an extremely versatile instrument and a great investment.

StingRay players

- Bernard Edwards (Chic)
- Flea (Red Hot Chili Peppers)
- John Deacon (Queen)
- Tony Levin (Alice Cooper, King Crimson, John Lennon, et al)

Choosing amps

An amplifier or "amp" can transform the feeble sound of an electric bass into a stomach-churning rumble.

Balancing your purchase

There is no point buying an expensive bass and plugging it into a cheap amp, or vice versa. When the first electric basses were produced, valve technology was king, and so all of the early amp designs were valve-based. While guitarists still love the sound of valve amps, most bass players prefer to use solid-state amplification because of the increased clean headroom it provides. While distortion sounds cool on guitar, it makes the bass sound muddy and unfocused, preventing it from locking tightly with the kick drum. What's more, a bass will swiftly kill the speakers in a guitar amp, so don't be tempted to plug into your mate's shiny new combo, or you could be presented with an eye-watering bill for new speakers!

The Laney RB1 Richter and the Marshall MB 15 are good-quality, reliable, reasonably-priced amps ideal for first-time buyers.

Top five beginner amps

1 Laney RB1 Richter

2 Ibanez SWX20

3 Fender Rumble 15

4 Marshall MB 15

5 Peavey MAX 158

The stack

The stack consists of an amplifier and one or two speaker cabinets. These rigs are extremely loud and heavy. In fact, they are really the preserve of the pro, touring musician who can afford the luxury of a road crew to lug this unwieldy bit of kit around.

The valve stack was extremely popular with rock bassists in the 1960s and early 1970s. Jack Bruce (Cream), Roger Glover (Deep Purple), and Andy Fraser (Free) were all early devotees of the Marshall 100-watt stack with a minimum of two 4x12 cabs. The Acoustic 360 bass stack was one of the earliest solid-state rigs that appeared in the early 1970s and was a familiar site at big gigs. Jaco Pastorious and John Paul Jones (Led Zeppelin) are just two of the many Acoustic bass rig devotees. The company went bankrupt in the 1980s, but were relaunched as Acoustic Amplification in 2007 with a brand new line of bass combos and stacks.

Some of the defining rock 'n' roll gigs of the last fifty years were performed in front of a wall of Marshall stacks.

The combo

Bass combo amplifiers first emerged in the early 1950s. They are smaller than the "stack," since the amp and speaker(s) are combined into a single cabinet. The Fender Bassman is probably the most famous of them all and was first introduced in 1952—it is still in production to this day in reissue form. All of the major manufacturers make a huge range of combo amps, from small practice amps, to backbreaking 100-watt monsters. Practice amps are extremely good value for money and much louder than their name suggests. Some manufacturers offer "beginner packages" that bundle the bass, amp, gig bag, and strap in one handy deal, and are very competitively priced. The downside is that you're limited to one manufacturer, so you won't have a great deal of choice.

Amp-modelling and computer software

Over the last decade or so, amp-modelling software such as "Guitar Rig" by Native Instruments (which includes bass amp models) or Ampeg SVX by IK Multimedia have become extremely popular for home recording enthusiasts with a computer-based setup. However, if you don't want to have to boot up your computer every time you want to practice, you could opt for a hardware version of amp-modelling (these have no speakers and need to be plugged into an external amplifier or headphones), like the Line 6 Bass Pod XT, or the Behringer Bass V-Amp. Both types of device are really designed for recording; there is no need to upset the neighbors by "cranking up" your amp to get a good sound. Most bass players steer clear of amp-modelling units when playing live—they are just too fiddly.

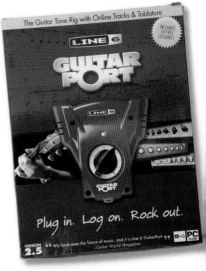

The headphone amp

Headphone amplifiers are ideal for quiet practice sessions and are relatively inexpensive. Some of these pocket-sized gadgets (like the Korg PX5D) even manage to pack in a very useable set of amp-modelled sounds: a drum machine, a tuner, and a time-stretching facility for slowing down those "hard to nail" bass licks! If you want to practice in complete privacy without disturbing anyone, these little gadgets are well worth a look. If you don't want all the bells and whistles included in Korg's PX5D, the Rockman Bass Ace and Dean's "Bass in a Box" headphone amps are well worth checking out.

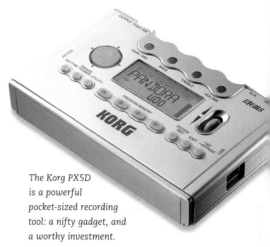

The Korg PX5D is a powerful pocket-sized recording tool: a nifty gadget, and a worthy investment.

It may be a little old-fashioned, but the headphone amp is ideal if you're practicing late at night and don't want to disturb slumbering neighbors, family, or flatmates.

Essential accessories

Once you're the proud owner of that shiny new bass, you'll soon realize that an accessory or two could come in handy. Some of these are optional items, such as a strap; others, like the tuner, are simply indispensable.

◀ Guitar tuners

These handy little devices are an absolute "must have," so if you buy only one thing from this list, make sure it's one of these. Most tuners are automatic, so all you have to do is plug in and tune up. Prices have fallen considerably in recent years with the influx of Eastern goods, so it won't cost you an arm and a leg either!

Metronome ▶

This may not seem like the most exciting accessory, but it's a must for the serious bass guitar student. Practicing with a metronome on a regular basis will help you to develop a good sense of time. It can take some players a long time to acknowledge the importance of this, so start now and get ahead of the competition.

◄ Guitar stands

Keeping your bass on a stand instead of in its case makes it easier to grab and play. Leaning your instrument against a chair is not a good idea—if it falls on the floor, the headstock could easily break or snap off. When you're taking a well-earned break from practice, a guitar stand will keep your bass safe.

Music stand ►

Once you've bought one of these, you'll wonder why you spent so long hunched over that book on your knees. The collapsible metal type is inexpensive and can be packed away easily for travel.

▲ Leads

If you've just bought an electric guitar "starter pack," then chuck that low-quality bundled lead away. Good leads aren't cheap, but the signal quality is far superior and they will last for years.

▶ Spare strings

Bass strings are quite hard to break due to their thickness. There's nothing worse, however, than not having any to hand when they do, so it's well worth keeping a spare set in your case.

◀ Guitar care

At the very least you will need a cloth to wipe your guitar strings when you've finished playing. This prolongs the life of the strings and prevents an unpleasant build up of grime—'nuff said! There's a wide range of guitar care products on the market: polish, fretboard cleaner, treatments to prolong string life, cleaning cloths, peg winders (to make light work of string changing), and more. All of them are designed to help you keep your guitar in tip-top condition.

▼ Cases

Most guitars come with a soft case that provides little protection for your bass. A well-padded "gig bag" is a good investment and allows you to carry your bass on your back like a rucksack, making light work of traveling to and from rehearsals and gigs.

▼ Straps

If you're itching to get out there and start gigging, invest in a good quality leather strap. A cheap strap will soon start to stretch, particularly at the points where it's attached to the guitar, making it potentially hazardous for your bass' health.

Glossary of bass guitar terms

arpeggio When the notes of a chord are played sequentially as opposed to simultaneously, an arpeggio is created. Any chord can be played as an arpeggio.

back beat A term used to describe the emphasis of the weak beats— two and four (in 4/4 time)—in popular music. This is usually emphasized by the drummer (on the snare drum), but can also be reinforced by the rhythm guitarist if necessary.

CAGED system A system that organizes the guitar's fingerboard into five regions based on the five open guitar chord shapes: C, A, G, E, and D. While these chord shapes are not used on the bass, the related arpeggio and scale patterns are.

consonance An interval or chord is described as being "stable" when consonant. This is created by the series of harmonic overtones that are produced when the notes are sounded simultaneously. A consonant chord or interval is used to release the tension created by dissonant chords and intervals.

damping When strings are muted by releasing the pressure of the fretting hand, or by touching the strings with the palm of the picking hand near the bridge, they are said to be damped.

diatonic The term is applied to any note, interval, or chord that occurs naturally in a major or minor key (i.e. without requiring any scale note to be changed with a sharp, flat, or natural).

dissonance The opposite of consonance, a dissonant chord or interval is said to be "unstable." Dissonance is used to create motion in harmony by creating a need for resolution. This is described as "tension and release;" the dissonance provides tension, which is released when consonance occurs.

dominant seventh A major chord or arpeggio with a fourth note added. The extra note must be a minor third above the fifth to create a minor seventh interval from the root note. The chord/ arpeggio occurs diatonically on the fifth (V or dominant) degree of the major scale, the harmonic and melodic minor scales, and resolves naturally to each scale's tonic (I). It is described as being dissonant because of the diminished fifth interval between the major third and minor seventh.

enharmonic A term used to describe a note, chord, key signature, or arpeggio that has an alternative letter spelling, e.g. F#/G♭ or B♭/A#.

fingerstyle The technique of plucking the strings with the first two fingers of the right hand as opposed to using a pick (plectrum). This technique produces a warmer sound than when playing with a plectrum (see "pickstyle").

hammer-on This is created when only the first of two notes on the same string is picked—the second note is produced by fretting the note sharply ("hammering" the finger onto the fretboard) without picking it. If the first note is not an open string, it must be fretted throughout.

Jazz fake books A fake book compacts tunes in a concise format using only the melody, chord changes, and often the lyrics, giving the player creative freedom.

legato A term that literally means to play smoothly or "tied together." Bassists achieve this by playing consecutive hammer-ons and pull-offs.

major A term used to describe a chord, arpeggio, interval, or key. The major chord is the most consonant (i.e. stable) chord in music. It is constructed from the first, third, and fifth degrees of the major scale. Major chords, arpeggios, intervals, and keys are often described as "happy"- sounding. Major intervals include the 2nd, 3rd, 6th, and 7th and are derived from the notes of the major scale.

minor A term used to describe a chord, arpeggio, interval, or key. The minor chord is slightly less consonant (i.e. less stable) than a major chord due to the relationship between the root note and the minor third. It is constructed from the first, third, and fifth degrees of the minor scale. Minor chords, arpeggios, intervals, and keys are described as "sad"-sounding. Minor intervals include the minor second, third, sixth, and seventh and are derived from the notes of the natural minor scale (i.e. aeolian mode).

moveable shape/pattern A riff, arpeggio, or interval that does not incorporate open strings and so can be played anywhere on the neck. Moveable shapes are very useful when "transposing" (moving to another key).

octave A term applied to an interval where the second note is eight notes (or 12 semitones) higher or lower and has the same letter name.

offbeat When counting in common time (4/4), the off-beats occur naturally between each beat. Counting "+" between the main beats will make it easier to locate the offbeats more accurately. A single bar of 4/4 would then be counted as "1 + 2 + 3 + 4 +."

open shape A riff, arpeggio, or interval played in first position and using open strings.

Paganini technique Instead of using separate fingers to play adjacent notes on the same fret, one finger is "rolled" across the strings to play both notes. The technique is named after its pioneer, the nineteenth century virtuoso violinist, Niccolò Paganini (see page 41 for more).

pickstyle A technique involving the use of a pick (plectrum) to sound the bass guitar's strings. The technique produces more attack and is ideal for rock and associated styles.

pick-up These are situated under the strings on the body of an electric bass, and "pick up" the vibrations of the strings. An electromagnetic device that essentially functions as a simple microphone, they convert the vibrations of each string into an electric signal, which is then amplified by a guitar amplifier or "amp."

positions (e.g. third position) This describes the position of the left hand on the fretboard. When playing in "first position," the first finger plays all notes on the first fret, the second finger all notes on the second fret, etc. So for "third position" the hand moves up the neck and the first finger now plays all notes on the third fret, the second finger plays notes on the fourth fret, etc.

power chord A guitar-specific, two-note chord that consists of a root note and a fifth. Sometimes the root note is doubled an octave higher to create a bigger sound. Since a power chord contains no third, it is neither major nor minor. The symbol "5" is used to denote a power chord (e.g. C5 = C power chord).

pull-off A pull-off is created when only the first of two notes on the same string is picked—the second note is produced by "flicking" the fretting finger slightly sideways as it is lifted off the string. If the second note is not an open string, it must be fretted throughout.

riff An ostinato (repeated) pattern, usually no more than two bars in length and often played on the lower strings of the bass. Pink Floyd's "Money" is a classic example of a song driven along by a hypnotic bass riff.

scale A series of stepwise ascending (and descending) notes that follow a specific intervallic template of whole (tone) and half steps (semitones). These are generally seven notes long (i.e. the major scale), but can be shorter (i.e. the five-note pentatonic), or longer (i.e. the eight-note diminished scale).

slide This is achieved by picking only the first note, and then sliding the fretting finger up or down the neck to a new location. The fretting finger must maintain pressure on the fingerboard when sliding or the second note will not sound.

slur A slur is written above or below notes on the stave (as a curved line) to indicate legato phrasing. Bass players achieve legato phrasing by using hammer-ons and pull-offs.

stave The stave or staff is a system of five lines used to denote pitch in conventional music notation. Specific symbols denote the length of each note or rest (silence).

syncopation The emphasis of "weak" beats to create an interesting rhythm. Weak beats occur on the second and fourth beat (in 4/4 time), or on an offbeat (i.e. occurring between the main beats).

TAB Originally used to notate lute music during the Renaissance period, this is a simplified form of notation that indicates where a note should be played on the fretboard. It does not indicate note duration or rests (silence).

tone/semitone The basic unit of measuring the distance between two notes. A tone is equivalent to a whole step (two frets) and a semitone a half step (one fret).

Index

Index

Fold-out flap

Use this handy pull-out guide
as a quick reference to the
symbols and terms used in
this book.

Anatomy of the bass guitar

Fret locator

Finding notes quickly on the fretboard
can be tricky. The blue circles here
indicate the fret number (for example,
1 = fret 1). Remember that after the
twelfth fret, the entire fingerboard
repeats an octave higher.

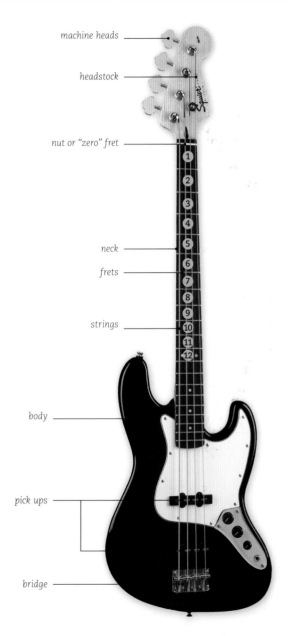

machine heads

headstock

nut or "zero" fret

neck

frets

strings

body

pick ups

bridge

Bass guitar: in a nutshell

This page contains essential information on reading music for bass guitar, and will help you find your way around the scale and arpeggio libraries.

Rhythmic notation

Bass guitar uses the rhythmic notation system, which describes rhythm but not pitch. Here are some of the different notes and symbols that you will encounter throughout this book.

Note		Value
◇	whole note	4 beats
♩	half note	2 beats
♩	quarter note	1 beat
♪	eighth note	½ beat
♬	16th note	¼ beat

Rest		Value
▬	whole rest	4 beats
▬	half rest	2 beats
𝄽	quarter rest	1 beat
𝄾	eighth rest	½ beat
𝄿	16th rest	¼ beat

Understanding the symbols used in the scale and arpeggio libraries (pages 166–233)

The scale and arpeggio patterns in this book are notated on a graphic TAB-style diagram. Below are some of the symbols you will encounter:

▪ *Red squares indicate the root notes in each example (e.g. all the Cs contained in a C major scale).*

① *The white circles clearly show where you should place your fingers, and the number indicates which finger should be used.*

7 *The number in the white square indicates the fretboard position.*

In addition to the boxed number, the handy fretboard locator defines the region of the neck that is used.

Picking symbols

⊓ = down-pick

V = up-pick

Finger symbols

i (*indice*) = index

m (*medio*) = middle

Credits

Quarto would like to acknowledge the following agencies:

- 16, 17, 54, 55, 68, 120, 121, 144, 145, 158, 159, 236: Redferns Music Picture Library
www.redferns.com
- Fold-out flap
www.shutterstock.com

We would like to thank the following companies for kindly supplying us with images:

- FENDER®, PRECISION BASS®, JAZZ BASS®, AFFINITY SERIES, RUMBLE, and the distinctive headstock and body designs of the FENDER instruments depicted herein are trademarks of Fender Musical Instruments Corporation and are used with permission.
- D'Addario & Co./ Katie Colleary, D'Addario
www.daddario.com
- Marshall Amplification plc.
www.marshallamps.com
- Laney Amplification
www.lanley.com
- Korg
www.korg.co.uk
- Ernieball
www.ernieball.com

We would also like to thank Nick Franks at Gibson for the loan of the Gibson EB/SG for photography:

Gibson Musical Instruments
29–35 Rathbone Street
London W1T 1NJ
Tel: 0044 20 7167 2143   Fax: 0044 20 7167 2150

Representing: Gibson, Epiphone, Baldwin, Kramer, Maestro, Slingerland, Tobias, Steinberger, Valley Arts, Wurlitzer and more. Visit: www.gibson.com